Wedding Occasions

101 NEW PARTY THEMES FOR WEDDING SHOWERS, REHEARSAL DINNERS, ENGAGEMENT PARTIES, AND MORE!

BY CYNTHIA LUECK SOWDEN

BRIGHTON PUBLICATIONS INC.

BRIGHTON PUBLICATIONS, INC.

Copyright © 1990 by Cynthia Lueck Sowden

Brighton Publications, Inc.
P.O. Box 12706
New Brighton, MN 55112
(612) 636-2220

First Edition: 1990

Library of Congress Cataloging-in-Publication Data
Sowden, Cynthia Lueck.
Wedding Occasions : 101 New Party Themes
for Rehearsal Dinners, Engagement Parties, and More
Includes Index
1. Wedding etiquette.
2. Weddings. I. Title.
BJ 2051.568   1990   90-1488
395'.22–dc20
ISBN 0-918420-10-5

Printed in the United States of America

Dedicated to my husband, Ralph, who encouraged me; my daughter, Beth, who colored her own "book"; and my mother, Iris Lueck, who did the ironing while I wrote this book.

Acknowledgments

Special thanks to the following people, whose talent, expertise and generous gift of time helped me complete this book:

Ralph Berlovitz, The Victorian Photographer

Kim Brown, Senior Account Manager, TravelCorp

Virgil Lamb, Meeting Planner and Convention Director, Lifetouch National School Studios Inc.

Nancy Larson, Director of Sales, The Hopkins House

Michael Macken, President, Macken Music and Entertainment Agency

Susan Meyer, Senior Account Executive, Arrowwood — A Radisson Resort

Sandy Neuwirth, Sales Manager, Bloomington Convention & Visitors Bureau

Lynn Shafer, Director of Sales, Outing Lodge at Pine Point, Stillwater, Minnesota

Debbie Van Ravenhorst, Administrative Sales Manager, Jostens

Laura Zahn, author of Room at the Inn: Guide to Historic B&Bs, Hotels and Country Inns Close to the Twin Cities, Room at the Inn Wisconsin and Wake Up and Smell the Coffee

and my good friend, Wendy Wurr, Director of Sales, Arrowwood — A Radisson Resort, for all her help in finding the right people to talk to.

Table of Contents

Introduction:

Wedding Occasions for Today's Couples

Through the centuries, wedding ceremonies have been constantly evolving. So, too, have the events and revelry that surround them.

Next to the wedding celebration, the shower is the most popular and often celebrated occasion. Today, although bridal showers are still popular, couples showers are becoming more common. The bridegroom is no longer left out of parties where gifts are given that benefit both him and the bride. Today's couples are celebrating *together*.

Today's couples are also celebrating more of the very special days before the wedding. Everything from announcing the engagement to fitting the gowns has become a reason to celebrate. A series of mini-events leads up to the Big Day.

Celebrations are lasting longer, too. They don't end with the last set of songs at the wedding dance. More and more couples are enjoying "weekend weddings" involving a number of events spread over a three-day period. Guests who travel long distances to attend the wedding are staying longer and appreciate being entertained as they renew old ties. Newlyweds are spending more time with their families before leaving for their honeymoon.

This book is designed to help you celebrate the occasions both before and after your wedding day. You can follow the 101 themes in these pages word for word, or you can use them as a departure point for a unique party of your own creation. Some of the themes are proven winners; others have been carefully thought through. Many are inexpensive; others will tax your budget a bit more. Many of these party ideas are interchangeable. "Heritage Rehearsal Dinner" could be used to welcome out-of-town guests just as well as the "Regional Buffet Bash."

To help you translate your ideas into reality, I have included much practical information gleaned from interviews with professionals who have experience working with brides and grooms. I've also included a chapter on where to find props, favors, and other items.

However you choose to celebrate your wedding day, you can make it even more joyous by turning the little events into an occasion, too. I hope this book will help you do just that.

Cynthia Lueck Sowden

1. Planning a Party

*E*ntertaining guests just seems to come naturally for some people: They know the right things to do and say to make their guests feel at home. Their decorations are inspired, the food plentiful and delicious. Their parties are always well attended and their guests long remember the good time they had.

There is a reason for the success of any party: planning. Good parties don't just happen. They're carefully orchestrated, right down to the smallest detail.

If you're not detail oriented, planning all the particulars of a party may sound like drudgery. But following a plan can relieve you of much of the drudgery and make things easier, because you move logically from one step to another. You're not flying off in several directions all at once.

When you plan an event, you need to consider several factors:

1. Purpose of the event: Are you announcing an engagement, giving a couples shower, or hosting weekend guests?

2. Number of guests: Are you planning a small, intimate dinner or a large gathering?

3. Location: Many homes cannot accommodate large groups. If you're planning a "Back to the Fifties Sock Hop" you'll need lots of room for dancing. For any event that involves dancing or large numbers of guests, you may need to consider renting a hall.

4. Budget: What can you afford? If you don't have much money, perhaps a friend can help you host a couples shower.

5. Time constraints: If your job keeps you busy all week, you might not want to give up an entire Saturday to cook a gourmet meal. Do you have time to shop for the food, prepare it, and make your home presentable for guests? If not, you may be better off hiring a caterer.

Party Planning Guide _____

Whatever kind of celebration you're planning, it pays to take it one step at a time. Start by drawing up a work sheet similar to this one:

Occasion: _____

Date: _____ Time: _____

Place: _____

Theme: _____

Number of Guests: _____

Food: Catered _____ Prepared by me_____

Music: Recorded _____ Live_____

Disc jockey _____

Photos: Professional _____ Taken by a friend_____

Decorations/Props needed: _____

Invitations:_____

Favors:_____

Parking: Off-street_____ Lot Cost_____

Activities: _____

_____

_____

Let's take a closer look at some of the key elements of party planning.

Budget

Unless you're independently wealthy, you'll need to establish a budget for your celebration. Remember, a budget will not affect the theme of your event. It *will* have a bearing on the way in which you spend your money to make your theme work.

Deciding in advance how much you can spend will help you make critical decisions such as whether to hire a disc jockey or a live dance band. Preparing a budget will show you where you can cut corners so that you can spend more money in other areas.

A budget also gives you a basis for negotiation when working with hotels, caterers, and so on. You'll make more of an impression (and get the supplier's immediate respect) when you say, "I want to spend $10 per person," rather than coming in with vague and unrealistic notions about serving a seven-course meal and then going into shock when the bill comes to $25 per plate.

Two of the biggest influences on your party budget are the number of guests and the location. If you're hosting 200 people, you'll need a large entertainment space. You'll also need a lot of food and beverages, and the money to pay for it all. On the other hand, a simple announcement party that includes only you and the groom, his parents, and your parents can take place comfortably in most apartment living rooms.

Likewise, if you're planning on having expensive entertainment — a live band or disc jockey, for example — you can count on spending more money than if you check a few records or tapes out from your local library.

Before you get too carried away with your party planning, do some preliminary checking on prices of various items. If you want to open your wedding gifts in a nearby park after the wedding, find out what it costs to rent a large, striped tent or canopy by calling two or three rental stores.

Another word of caution: The lowest price may not always be the best value. One rental agency's tents may show more wear and tear than another's. Don't automatically rule out a live band in favor of a disc jockey just because you've heard that D.J.s charge less — the price difference may be negligible.

As you compare prices, put your findings in a log like this one:

	Location #1	Location #2	Location #3
Room rental			
Food			
Bar			
Entertainment			
Decorations			
Miscellaneous			

This budget exercise will be extremely helpful to you if someone is helping you pay for the party. Traditionally, the groom's friends pay for the bachelor party and his family, the rehearsal dinner. The bride's family takes care of the brides-maids' luncheon and wedding reception. It all boils down to who will or can bear the expense. If a favorite aunt offers to give a shower, perhaps she can be persuaded to host the bridesmaids' luncheon instead.

Location

The size of your guest list will determine your space requirements.

An American Legion, VFW, or similar type of hall provides a lot of room for dancing. Compared to a country club, a hall of this type may be inexpensive to rent, and may give you more flexibility with booking dates. You may be able to bring in your own food. Since many of these halls are plain rooms with tile floors and concreteblock walls, you'll have to work harder on decorations. One plus is that parking generally is ample.

A hotel will have a smaller dance floor but will probably offer a more elegant atmosphere. And you'll receive more service. Prices will be higher, but parking should be no problem. Most hotels will not allow you to bring your own food or beverages. On the other hand, you may get some assistance with room decorations.

A bed-and-breakfast establishment is a smaller, owner-occupied inn, often with no more than ten sleeping rooms. Some larger inns can accommodate large groups such as weddings and wedding receptions; others are best limited to small gift-opening parties or rehearsal dinners. Service is extremely personal. Because the B&B is more like your own home, all you may need for decorations are a few bouquets or candles. Many B&Bs are furnished with fragile antiques and do not welcome children. B&Bs are frequently found in residential areas, so parking may be a problem for larger parties. They often have to comply with local noise ordinances, and cannot allow loud parties. A restaurant may be an ideal location for a smaller gathering — although some may be able to accommodate a sizeable group. You can expect good service and adequate parking. Decorating needs may be minimal; a centerpiece for the head table may be all you need to provide.

If your party includes outdoor activities such as water-skiing or tennis, you will, of course, need to hold the party in an outdoor area near a lake or tennis courts. Be sure to have adequate shelter for your guests if the weather suddenly changes from fair to foul.

A resort may be the ideal wedding weekend location for an active family. Golf, tennis, horseback riding, and swimming are all in one place! Many resorts also offer children's activities and baby-sitting services that allow adults to pursue their own interests.

As the party giver, you are responsible for making sure that ample parking is available for your guests. Whether you live on a busy thoroughfare or on a quiet cul-de-sac, make arrangements with your neighbors or the police to ensure that your guests' vehicles will be safe while they are attending your party.

Themes

Can you have a party that doesn't have a theme? Of course you can! A theme is merely a tool you use to help you plan the party. Although you could give a theme party just to do a theme party, have a *reason* for using a specific theme.

Themes actually give you more control over the event you're staging because they give you a clear direction in which to plan. A "Gourmet Cooking Party" is much more specific than a simple kitchen shower. Once you've chosen your theme, you can follow it to its conclusion.

Themes also attract guests. Instead of calling up a few friends and saying, "I'm going to have a couples shower for Candy and Brian Friday night. Bring a present," you can send out invitations with some pizzazz. Your guests will know immediately that a Western Shower is going to be more interesting than a run-of-the-mill towels and linen shower. They'll come out of curiosity, if nothing else.

Themes can help you plan activities. If you live in snow country and you're hosting guests from warmer climes, you can build a party around the weather in your area. Similarly, if your guests come from many different parts of the country, you can plan activities to help them mingle and get to know one another. Themes can also help you build camaraderie among members of the wedding party who may not have met before.

You can shop for decorations with your theme in mind. A "Halloween Shower" just wouldn't be right without a jack-o'-lantern or two. And what's a "Prom Night" engagement party without a mirror ball to cast spinning reflections around the room?

Themes also give you an advantage in coming up with a gift or favor for your guests to take home as a remembrance of the occasion. Whether it's a T-shirt or a pair of earrings, your guests should be able to look at the favor and say, "Oh, that's a favor from Stacy's bridesmaids' luncheon."

A theme banquet or dinner is much more fun than an ordinary sit-down dinner. Which would you rather go to: a dinner party in an elegant restaurant, or a dinner party in an elegant restaurant where you are serenaded by strolling minstrels dressed in medieval costumes?

Use your theme to shape your menu, too. A Western theme party is more likely to include chili and biscuits than liver paté and caviar.

You can use the party themes in this book exactly as they are described or you can change and embellish them in any way you desire. For additional help in getting theme ideas, talk to the catering manager of the hotel or facility where you're holding your party. Hotels that host many business meetings frequently stage themed mini-events such as coffee or refreshment breaks. Perhaps the catering manager at the hotel would be willing to set up a similar program for you.

Guest List

The primary reason for making a guest list is to remind yourself to invite everyone you really want to have at your party. There are several ways to make a guest list. One way is to just write the names and addresses of all the guests down on a piece of paper. A more efficient method is to purchase some ruled 3½" x 5" cards at an office-supply store and write the name and address of each guest on a separate card. File the cards in alphabetical order in a recipe file box. To aid you in this task, you can also get alphabetic dividers at the office-supply store.

As the responses come in, you can quickly find the names of the respondents and place a little check mark next to their names. This method is particularly effective for brides who are preparing their wedding guest list. After the wedding, you can use the cards to keep track of your holiday card list.

When you're throwing a party such as a shower or rehearsal dinner, be sure to ask the bride or groom about any special guests, such as grandmothers or aunts, whom they may want to include.

Invitations and RSVPs

Invitations set the tone for the entire party. A clever invitation piques curiosity, provides a spark, and gives your guests an idea of what's to come. An invitation with attractive graphics and artwork will excite your guests. They'll perceive your party as an event they won't want to miss!

If you can afford it, of course, you can hire a professional designer to create a cover design, select the style of type, pick out ink colors and get the invitations printed for you. It is also perfectly proper to use preprinted, fill-in-the-blank form invitations for almost any wedding-related party. However, it's really more fun — and not very difficult — to make your own. If you have a personal computer, you can use any number of inexpensive software programs to design your own invitations. You can take the finished art to an instant printer, or you can copy the invitations on a photocopy machine.

If you enjoy cutting and pasting, you can make inexpensive and very effective invitations from construction paper, glue, glitter, swatches of material — you name it.

If you're a calligrapher, you can give your party invitations an elegant look with a few deft strokes of the pen. Experiment with gold or silver ink on dark-colored papers.

Look for unusual ways to announce your party. The invitation can be printed on beach balls or ears of dried corn which are mailed in cardboard tube. A note can be wrapped around an artist's paintbrush. A brown paper bag can bear the printed party information on the outside. If you do decide to use a preprinted form invitation, liven it up with some metallic sprinkles that fall out of the card when it's opened.

And who's to say that only written invitations are acceptable? Record your party invitation on cassette tapes and mail them to your guests. You're limited only by your imagination!

Because good communication is essential to a party's success, a good invitation must provide certain basic information to your guests:

1. What is your party's objective? Are you having an engagement party? A couples shower? A rehearsal dinner?

2. Who is hosting the event? You? You and a friend?

3. Where will the party be held? If you've given parties and nobody came, maybe it's because you forgot to give them the address of the restaurant or home.

4. What are the date and time? Let your guests know when they're expected to arrive.

5. Will the party be held in an unusual or out-of-the-way location? If so, give directions on how to get there. Provide a detailed map, either on the back of the invitation or inserted into the envelope with it. Be sure to tell guests where they can park their cars. If parking will cost money, be sure to let your guests know that, too.

6. Are guests required to bring something or wear special attire? If you are having a "Cupid's Temple of Love" party, for example, tell your guests to bring valentines. If you are having a "Midwinter Beach Party," remind them to bring their bathing suits.

7. Will the party feature special cuisine? If you are hosting a "Heritage Rehearsal Dinner," you may want to list the menu items as an extra enticement to come.

Send out invitations in a timely manner. Give people at least two weeks to work your party into their schedules. Don't assume that their calendars are open.

If your invitation requires an RSVP (French for "Please respond"), mail your invitations out early enough so that your guests have time to reply. People tend to get confused about RSVPs, so be specific; set a time limit within which they must respond.

Don't be surprised if guests who never responded show up at the party, and those who said they'd be coming never make it. It's a fact of party life.

If the group is small and you know that most of the people you've invited will attend, you can tell them to "RSVP regrets only" and give them a telephone number where they can reach you. You can also accept phoned RSVPs for larger groups.

If you're expecting a large crowd for a function such as an engagement party and you need a head count for the caterer, then consider printed cards. The cards should ask for guests' responses by a certain date, and the envelopes for the cards should be addressed to you and stamped. Your guests should not have to pay postage.

An RSVP could read like this:

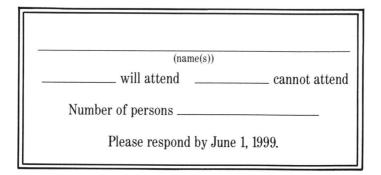

Activities

Although adults often groan at the mere mention of playing games, the wise hostess or host schedules fun activities during the course of the party. Activities keep the party going and give guests something to talk about.

If your guests don't know each other, provide mixer activities that will help them get to know one another. Even the most standoffish adults will play games such as Trivial Pursuit™ and Pictionary™.

Ideally, your activities will tie into your party theme. For example, a "Slippin' and Slidin' Party" will include ice skating and tobogganing. A "Look to the Future" will feature a fortune teller or psychic.

Activities should also take the guests into consideration. For a couples shower, for example, you'll need to think of activities that males and females can do together. A younger crowd would appreciate a fast-paced game of volleyball. If your guest list includes several persons from the older generation, you may want to schedule less strenuous activities such as a leisurely game of croquet.

Make sure you begin your activities right away so that the party theme is carried throughout the party.

Food and Beverages

The great thing about food is that it's so versatile. From a simple stew to an elegantly sculpted butter centerpiece, food is the most flexible medium a party planner can use. Food ties easily into a theme party. What menu could be easier to plan than a "Friday Night Fiesta," complete with tostadas, refried beans, nachos, and margaritas? Seafood is a natural at a "Pirate's Beach Party."

Food is also wonderfully flexible in the ways in which it can be presented. You can treat your guests to a sit-down dinner, a buffet, or "food stations," where they go from table to table selecting different food items or courses. You can present a dainty afternoon tea or a picnic in the park.

Use food to highlight regional cuisine. Prepare the dishes your area is famous for. Celebrate your family's ethnic heritage by serving dishes handed down from generation to generation.

Kitchens are traditional gathering places at any party. So have the party in the kitchen! Getting guests involved in the preparation of the meal provides entertainment for them while it cuts down on the amount of work you have to do.

Prepare enough food so that guests go away feeling satisfied. If the food is good and plentiful, your guests will remember your party and your generosity.

Food need not be accompanied by alcoholic beverages. The thoughtful hostess supplies plenty of alternatives. Always make sure you have coffee, soft drinks, and non-alcoholic punch or mineral water on hand for guests who may be acting as the designated driver or who simply do not want to drink.

Many persons have dietary restrictions that were not common a few years ago. In addition to religious restrictions, people are also more conscious of food allergies, cholesterol levels, and salt or sugar intake. Thoughtful hostesses who are aware of these restrictions try to accommodate their guests. If you want to avoid offending anyone, you can follow the lead of savvy New York caterers:

≈ Avoid shellfish, pork, duck, lamb, and fried foods.

≈ Focus on vegetables and salads.

≈ Serve plenty of starches such as potatoes, bread, or pasta.

≈ Try to cook without butter, animal fats, eggs, and salt. Use a variety of herbs and spices to flavor your dishes.

≈ Go ahead and serve rich, heavy dessert — but also offer fresh fruit as an alternative.

≈ Always offer guests mineral water as well as their choice of regular or decaffeinated coffee.

Above all, don't be offended if a guest refuses a certain dish you've prepared — and don't press her to take a second helping or a dessert she doesn't want.

Decorations

Not every party requires elaborate decorations. You can create a festive atmosphere with a colored paper tablecloth and contrasting paper plates.

On the other hand, decorations reinforce your theme. They transform an ordinary living room into Cupid's temple of love. They help create a mood. A psychic's revelations may seem too public in a brightly lit room. Let her consultations take place on a more intimate level by keeping the lights turned low.

Decorations don't have to be expensive. Sure, you can rent potted palms for a "Midwinter Beach Party." You can also get the same summery effect by blowing up a few beach balls and placing them around the perimeter of a hotel pool.

Free up your imagination when you think about decorating the party area. Don't settle for a few balloons and streamers when candles in hurricane lamps and strings of tiny Christmas lights can turn your backyard into a summer fairyland.

If you're holding your party in a rented facility such as a hotel, be sure to tell the catering manager about your party theme. The hotel may have some props on hand that you can use to create the proper atmosphere. Pay particular attention to tabletops, but remember that you don't have to use fine linen, china and crystal to set a beautiful table! Old quilts, wool blankets, braided cotton rugs, and Oriental rugs make fine table coverings that give your guests something to talk about. Antique dresser scarves can do double duty as table runners.

Napkins are a versatile tabletop decoration. They can be folded and rolled into many shapes that will correspond beautifully with your party theme. If you're giving a "Friday Night Fiesta," you can use a Mexican fan fold (it even works with paper napkins!). For a "Heritage Rehearsal Dinner" that features a French menu, try a fleur-de-lis fold. (For a complete, easy-to-follow, step-by-step guide to napkin folding, consult Folding Table Napkins by Sharon Dlugosch, Brighton Publications, Inc., P. O. Box 12706, New Brighton, MN 55112.)

Let your imagination run free when you consider centerpieces. Don't settle for a traditional carnation-in-a-bud-vase centerpiece. Use unusual containers such as copper tea kettles, pumpkins, or an old high-topped shoe with a glass jar hidden inside. Or try a piece of firewood drilled with holes. Place florist's vials inside the holes to make a unique floral arrangement. A basket of pine cones makes a wonderful Christmas centerpiece if you tie a red and green plaid ribbon on the handle. Leave the cones in their natural state, or spray them with "snow."

Favors

Are favors necessary? No, but like an after-dinner mint, they leave a good taste in your guest's mouth. Favors are keepsakes that remind guests of the good time they had at your party. They're a thoughtful gesture that makes guests feel welcome and makes them want to return to sample your hospitality again and again.

Favors can be useful or frivolous. They don't have to be fancy or expensive — just a little something guests can take home with them. Like the decorations and the invitations, favors should reflect the theme of the party.

For instance, if you're sponsoring a "Saturday Softball Tournament," favors could be T-shirts or cheerleaders' pompoms. At an "Aviator's Rehearsal Dinner," use model airplanes as place-card holders — and as take-home gifts. A seed corn cap is just the thing to help guests remember a "Down-Home Rehearsal Dinner."

Photos — particularly the instant kind — make wonderfully versatile favors, particularly at dress-up affairs such as a "Halloween Shower" or "Prom Night" engagement party. Snap a picture of each guest as he or she enters the party room, then use the photo as a place card at the dinner table. Later, the picture can go home as a party favor.

Seasonal or holiday favors always work well. Jelly beans in small straw baskets for a springtime celebration, sunglasses for a summer party, or a packet of seeds "for growing good memories" are easy, fun mementos.

Food can also be used as a favor. Candy valentine hearts for an engagement party or liqueur-filled chocolates for a "Stock-the-Wine-Cellar Shower" make an edible remembrance of your party.

You can also present favors in a form that reminds guests of the theme. For example, the perfect favor for a "Wedding-Planning Party" might be a small calendar with all the important dates and times for showers, fittings, and so on already filled in for your attendants.

When you plan your party, be sure to consider budget, location, theme, guest list, invitations, activities, food, decorations. and favors. You'll find that the job of preparing for the party goes much more smoothly. With so much work done in advance, the party will take care of itself.

So get busy and start planning!

2. Working with Suppliers

*E*ngagement parties, showers, rehearsal dinners. For many, it's the first time they've ever planned any kind of event, large or small.

Unless you make your living planning corporate meetings or events, you probably haven't had much experience working with restaurants or caterers. Hiring musicians may seem like stepping onto foreign soil. Hoteliers may sound as though they're speaking another language.

It's easy to get confused when things don't go the way you think they should. Knowing what to expect can make working with these professionals much easier.

You may be surprised to learn that some suppliers regard wedding-party givers with something less than enthusiasm.

To you, your engagement party, rehearsal dinner, or weekend wedding may be the event of a lifetime. To them, it's business as usual — with an inexperienced, perfectionistic party planner, to boot.

Keep in mind that while you may have the perfect party mapped out in small detail in your mind, the people who will supply the labor, materials, food, banquet rooms, and so on, don't have X-ray eyes. They can't share your vision. Furthermore, each has her own way of doing business. Some have to follow the policies of large corporations and therefore must impose some limitations on your plans. Be flexible. Expect to do some negotiating, but don't be intimidated. After all, it's *your* money and *your* party.

Cost

The mistake made most often by novice party planners is blurting out, within minutes of meeting the hotel catering manager, "How much will it cost?" While it's understandable that you're concerned about costs, you need to provide the supplier with some basic information before he or she can answer your question.

Start by checking out two or three different locations for your party. Make sure they're available on the date you have chosen. Some country clubs may be booked as much as two or three years in advance. Hotels, on the other hand, may not want to book your event more than three months ahead of time. A popular restaurant may need only two or three weeks' notice.

How many are on your guest list? Even a rough count will help determine the size of the room you'll need to accommodate all your guests comfortably.

How much do you want to spend? If you've gone through the budget exercises in Chapter 1, you'll know where you stand.

Do you want to have an open bar and pay for all the cocktails your guests consume, or do you want to have a cash bar and let your guests buy their own drinks?

Earn the supplier's respect by doing your homework before you present yourself in his or her office.

Party Rooms

When you're shopping around for a place to hold your party, get all the information you can about each facility. Ask the catering manager or director of sales for an information packet. Included in the packet should be sample menus and food prices; catering policies; room rates; a room-layout guide, with seating capacity listed for each room; and perhaps a payment schedule if yours is to be a large or costly function.

Be sure to inquire about the type of business the hotel or resort caters to most frequently. Is it a family, social business, or convention hotel? A hotel that is used primarily as a social gathering place may be preferable to a convention hotel. If a convention is booked at the same time as your party, the hotel may assign your space to the convention-goers and you may find yourself scrambling for a party room.

Once you've signed a contract with the hotel, the hotel is legally bound to hold the space for you. If your party is asked to move, the hotel should help you find a new place to hold the party and give you some compensation for your trouble.

Some hotels book their meeting and banquet rooms as much as a year and a half in advance. Generally, however, most do not confirm dates until three months prior to the occasion.

Check out the grounds carefully. If any elderly people or persons with physical disabilities will be attending your party, make sure there are access ramps or ground-level doorways on the outside of the building, as well as elevators inside.

Make a note of the room capacity and seating arrangements. Although round tables allow for a more conversational atmosphere, they actually seat fewer people than eight-person, rectangular tables. If a bar and a head table will be part of the room setup, be sure to allow extra space for them. If dancing is on the agenda, make sure the room can accommodate all your friends and relatives and still leave plenty of room for dancing.

Many establishments do not allow you exclusive use of their pool for an entire evening. At best, you may be able to have the pool to yourselves for one hour.

Room rates vary according to the season and the popularity of the dates chosen. September, October, and May are the most popular wedding months. Not surprisingly, it's harder to book a party room during those months. Many bed-and-breakfast establishments do not allow you to book for more than two nights during the busy season.

On the other hand, you have more room for negotiation during less popular times. Ask the resort or hotel what its slow times are. For example, business is typically very slow in November, December and January. You may be able to negotiate a good price during the "dead" period between Christmas and New Year's Day. You may also be able to get a good bargain by booking your party on a Friday or Sunday evening.

Most facilities require a deposit on the banquet room. Depending on the policy of the individual hotel, the deposit may or may not be refundable. Be sure to ask about cancellation policies.

Find out which hotel services are free and which ones you could be charged for. For example, most hotels, because of dram shop laws, do not allow you to bring liquor into their facilities. Those that do, however, may charge a corkage fee to serve the liquor to your guests. Similarly, some hotels may charge a fee to cut the cake at your wedding reception, while others do it for nothing. Some Jewish celebrations may require a table of specially prepared foods. Sometimes the rabbi must bless the hotel ovens to make the food kosher. Be sure to ask if your rabbi will be allowed in the kitchen. Sometimes members of the family must prepare special foods. If the food is catered from a firm not associated with the hotel, the hotel may add a surcharge to the bill.

The establishment automatically sets the fee for tips and gratuities. The money doesn't necessarily all go to the waiters, waitresses, and other people working at the banquet. It may also be divided among the people who set up the tables and the catering staff, or it may used as a damage deposit on the room itself.

Food and Beverages

Although food can be quite expensive and overpriced, in general it is not a big money maker for hotels. Restaurants generally make a profit of about 15 cents on the dollar on food. Dinners served at a hotel already have much of the costs included in them.

The catering manager should give you a complete list of banquet, hors d'ouevres, and buffet menus. You should also receive a copy of the establishment's catering policies.

The following is a list of policies you should pay special attention to:

1. The meal guarantee. Most places want you to make your menu selection at least two weeks prior to the event. A guest count will be expected 24 to 48 hours before the actual date. This number is not usually subject to reduction. If fewer guests attend than you expect, you'll still be charged for the guaranteed amount.

   Do not make the mistake of ordering more food than you need. Most establishments are prepared to serve 5 to 10 percent more people than you guarantee in the guest count. Many times, especially in summer, about 5 percent of the people who say they are coming to your party fail to arrive. If you want to break even, you might give the catering manager a figure 5 percent lower than the actual number of expected guests.

Talk to the catering manager about leftovers; you may be able to take them home.

2. Cancellation charges. If you decide to cancel your event less than 30 days before the event (depending on the facility), you may be charged for rental of the room, whether you use it or not. At the very least, you may have to pay a cancellation penalty.

3. Bar tab. If you have a cash bar, the facility may waive the bartender's fee if you have a specified dollar amount in bar receipts. If your bar bill doesn't run that high, expect to pay a fee for the bartender in addition to the bill for the drinks. If you're picking up the tab, expect to tip the bartender. Some places also charge a gratuity on punch, wine, or kegs of beer.

4. Room rental fee. Most hotels have a banquet room charge, which may be waived if your party is larger than a certain minimum number of guests. If your party has less than the specified number of guests — 25, for example — you may be charged for the use of the banquet room in addition to the number of meals served.

5. Bill payment. Most places want to be paid in advance or on the day of the function. If you need to make credit arrangements, do so when you go over the contract with the catering manager.

Here are some other food facts to keep in mind:

1. Hors d'ouevres are expensive. Why? Because they require a lot of preparation, and you need five to seven different items to satisfy all your guests.

   Most establishments price their cold hors d'ouevres by the tray and their hot hors d'ouevres by the piece (usually with a minimum number of pieces). If you order appetizers in addition to a meal, many of them will be wasted. Allow six servings per person if you are beginning the evening with a cocktail hour. If the appetizers *are* the meal, allow ten to fifteen pieces per person.

2. Buffet meals are more expensive than are meals served at table. Why? Because of the preparation time required. Also, more food tends to be wasted with a buffet. A much larger variety and at least one-third more food must be prepared because buffets are a one-stop, all-you-can eat, serve-yourself dinner. Two entrees, a variety of salads, and several desserts must be offered.

3. Some places include dessert with the meal. To be sure, ask.

4. You should be able to sample the food that is to be served at your function. Make arrangements with the catering manager well in advance so that you can make any needed menu changes in a timely manner.

5. Champagne fountains are beautiful and elegant, but they tend to take the bubbles out of the bubbly, and they don't keep the champagne at the proper temperature. Fruit punches clog the fountain. To be elegant, yet keep costs down, have a waiter serve the champagne. There will be less waste, because guests will be less likely to walk away from a half-empty glass and get another one. Expect a small charge for the waiter service.

   Another way to make an elegant statement is to use an ice carving instead of a fountain. If the establishment cannot provide one for you, contact a local vocational-technical school that offers chef training. You may be able to purchase a student carving for a small fee. Be sure to clear it with the catering manager before you bring it to the party.

6. A cash bar, where guests pay for their own drinks, is less expensive than an open, or "hosted," bar. If you'd like to provide some type of alcoholic beverage, a carafe of wine on the table is usually adequate. When budgeting for beverages, plan about two drinks per person per hour at the price of a beer or house cocktail. House liquors are less expensive than "call" brands. (If you know that some of your guests prefer a certain brand, be sure to ask the catering manager to stock that brand as a courtesy to your guests.)

7. Hotels and restaurants make more money on alcohol than on food. There are several ways of charging for alcohol:
   a. By the bottle. By this method, a full bottle is pro-rated to the nearest tenth. The contents are measured, and you are charged for the amount of alcohol consumed.
   b. Per drink. Many bars now have fully programmed cash registers. All the bartender does is punch in "scotch and soda" and the cash register rings up the proper amount.
   c. Per shot. If you're ordering a mixed drink, you're paying double for your drink, although the bartender may allow you more than one ounce per shot. Drinks served "on the rocks" are always more expensive than those served "straight up."

8. Because of dram shop laws, self-serve bars and kegs of beer are becoming a thing of the past. No establishment wants to be held liable for allowing a patron to become drunk and later cause a car accident. Similarly, food brought in from the outside, other than a wedding cake, is generally banned from hotels and restaurants because eating establishments do not want to be held liable for a food poisoning incident.

When you're having a party catered, make sure you're working with a licensed company. If the catering operation has a current license, then you know it has undergone a routine inspection by the local health department. If the food is to be prepared at the catering operation, inspect the caterer's kitchen yourself for cleanliness. Refrigeration should be adequate, and there should be separate areas for handling raw and cooked foods.

Cold foods should be kept below 40 degrees Farenheit to maintain freshness. Hot foods should be kept at 140 degrees or higher. During the party, cold foods should be kept cold on a bed of crushed ice. Chafing dishes keep hot foods at the proper temperature.

Leftovers can be divided into small portions for quick freezing, or refrigerated for use within a day or two. Be sure to discuss what is to be done with leftovers with the caterer before you sign the contract.

Music

Music provides a beat for dancing and fills lulls in the conversation. It's a pleasant backdrop during dinner, and a mood-setter. Good music keeps the party going; poorly chosen or poorly performed music sends guests home early.

By all means, hire musicians for your rehearsal dinner. It will help break the ice if you're bringing two families together for the first time. The background supplied by a single pianist or harpist adds a nice touch and becomes a helpful conversation piece in a sometimes socially challenging situation.

Finding the right type of music for your event should not be difficult. First of all, decide whether your theme calls for live or recorded music. If records or tapes will do, go to your nearest public library and browse through its music section. You should be able to find everything from classics to jazz, from folk songs to New Wave.

If you decide that your party needs the energy provided by live musicians or a disc jockey and you have the money to pay for it, by all means, hire the best you can afford.

Begin your search with a trip through the Yellow Pages. Under "Musicians," you'll find listings for booking agencies. Why should you go through an agent? Wouldn't it be easier and less expensive to book the musicians directly? No!

Individual groups or musicians seldom advertise in the Yellow Pages because it is very costly. An agent can help you find just the right type of music for your function, whether it's a harpist, an ethnic group, a classical ensemble, or a Dixieland band. You should seriously question the musical quality of a group that books on its own. The group may be just getting started. And a group that books through an agent but takes jobs on the side isn't too concerned about ethics — or future business.

Working through an agency makes the best use of your time. An agency allows you to preview as many musicians as you like, without making you run all over town. Unless you have unlimited free time and can afford to spend your evenings traipsing from bar to bar auditioning groups, an agent is your best resource. In addition to audiotapes, many agents now have videotapes that allow you to see the musicians or D.J.s at work.

Do some basic homework before you decide to use a particular agent. How long has the agency been in business? Get referrals from other people who have used the agency. When you're working with a hotel or caterer, ask them for referrals. Many agents are in the business because they themselves are musicians. Be sure to ask if the agency specializes in supplying music for weddings and other special events, or if it books nightclub acts.

Musicians who work primarily at private functions are most likely to be booked in April, May, June, August, September, and October. The months from November through March are slower.

Be sure to tell your agent about your party theme. You'll want just enough theme music to establish your theme, and then you can switch to other types of music. If the band serves up a steady diet of polkas, you may alienate the guests who don't care for ethnic music. If there's a good variety of music, guests will stay longer and there's a good chance that the band will play some music they like. Think about the preferences of all your guests; don't pick only the music you yourself like.

Also think about the function itself. Do you want to provide an opportunity for lots of dancing? If so, then don't hire a blues artist. Like jazz, it's great music to listen to, but it's almost impossible to dance to.

When hiring a dance band, auditions are more critical than if you're seeking background music. Be sure to inquire about the group's experience. How long have the members been playing together? Do they play a variety of songs? What is the quality of their music? Ask for references from other clients.

If your party will be spread out over several rooms, as in a bed-and-breakfast establishment, or split between two locations such as the hotel pool area during the first hour and its ballroom for the rest of the evening, consider hiring strolling musicians. Here is a rule of thumb for maintaining a sense of balance between live musicians and the number of guests at a party:

❧ A three-piece group works well for up to 200 people.

❧ If the crowd is larger than 200, use a four- or five-piece ensemble.

Don't make the mistake of booking the least expensive act you can find. You get what you pay for. Most bands belong to the musicians union, but don't worry about paying union scale. This doesn't make the band more expensive. It's really a minimum-wage type of safety valve that prevents band leaders from starting price wars and putting themselves out of business.

Although disc jockeys often charge less than a live band, good ones cost just as much as a three-piece orchestra.

How do you recognize a good D.J.? The D.J. should entertain you with more than just musical selections. Look for an act that uses stage lighting skillfully. Because most D.J.s work alone, they have to have good special effects to establish a stage presence.

If you can see the D.J. in action, watch how he or she works with the crowd. Like any good bandleader, an experienced D.J. can "read" a room. He knows how to get the party going and keep it going — and how to cool things down if they get too hot. Check out the equipment, too. There's as much variety in equipment for D.J.s as there is in home stereos.

If you see a D.J. you like at a party, and want to make sure he'll perform at yours, ask him how you can "name-book" him. Many booking agencies have ten to twenty different disc jockeys working for them and will send out whoever is available on the night of your party. Unless you specify "Jumpin' Jack Flash," you might wind up with "Smokeless Joe."

Many bands now come equipped with break tapes, which

they play while they take a short rest between sets. If you prefer silence between sets, so your guests have a chance to visit, be sure to tell the bandleader.

Bands and D.J.s should always take requests. This special consideration makes people feel welcome at the party. Keep in mind, however, that within a given four-hour period, about 48 tunes will be played (roughly twelve an hour), so it may not be possible to honor every request.

When you hire performers, be sure to get everything in writing:

1. If you are hiring a band, specify the number of musicians. If you want to hire a specific D.J., be sure to specify that person by name.

2. Specify the date and time of the performance.

3. Specify the site.

4. Be sure to specify what kind of dress the performers should wear. Do you want them to wear tuxedos? If it's a country-Western band, clean blue jeans are appropriate.

5. Specify the number of hours for which you'll require music, and any provisions that must be made if the musicians are asked to work overtime.

6. If it isn't in the contract, write in a sentence that you, the purchaser, have control over the volume at which the music is performed. Also find out the power requirements of the band. Some groups need 220 amps instead of the usual 110. Most hotels charge an extra fee if they must bring in an electrician to increase the electrical service.

7. Specify the terms of payment.

Here is an example of a contract:

Contract No. _____

This agreement is null and void unless signed and

returned by:_____

Date Mailed: _____

1. Date of Contract:_____

2. Name and Address of Place of Engagement:_____

_____

_____

3. Name of Band or Act:_____

4. No. of Musicians: _____

5. Date(s), Starting and Finishing of Engagement: _____

_____

_____

6. Type of Engagement: _____

7. Total Compensation: _____

8. Purchaser will make payments as follows: _____

_____

_____

9. The agreement of the musicians to perform is subject to proven detention by sickness, accidents, riots, strikes, epidemics, acts of God, or any other legitimate conditions beyond their control.

_____   _____
Purchaser's name   Name of Band or Act

_____   _____
Signature   Signature

Address _____   _____
                                Engagement accepted by
_____   (Agent's name)

Phone _____

Decorating

In Chapter 3 of this book are suggested sources for some of the decorations mentioned in the party theme chapters that follow. Here are some additional tips on room decoration and props:

1. If your party will be held in a hotel, you may not have much time to decorate. If the room is being used for a function earlier in the day, you may have only an hour or two to put up your decorations after the hotel crew has reset the room. (Resetting takes one to two hours, depending on the size of the room and the configuration of tables and chairs.) The crew should be able to help you with heavy or difficult decorating jobs.

2. The hotel or restaurant may have candleholders you can use if you bring your own candles.

3. Find out whether the facility provides floral arrangements, and what kind. Some restaurants or hotels may put a single carnation on each table, whereas a bed-and-breakfast may grace each table with a lavish bouquet.

4. When renting props for your party, be sure to look at what you're getting; don't choose a prop on the basis of a photograph or drawing. One meeting planner thought she was renting a lovely grove of live, potted palms. They turned out to be wooden sticks topped with paper "leaves."

5. Many B&Bs are tastefully decorated. You may need to supply only a few bouquets or floral wreaths to make the atmosphere more festive. One bride placed peach-colored votive candles in every nook and cranny of the B&B where she held her reception.

Guest Accommodations

The rise in popularity of the wedding weekend, in which guests come early and stay beyond the ceremony, has created new duties and worries for the families of the bridal couple. After all, if Uncle Ray and Aunt Pat have traveled half a continent to get to your wedding, you can't ignore them! If you have the room, of course, you can put them up at your house. If you cannot, or if your guest list includes many out-of-town visitors, you should reserve a block of rooms at a local hotel.

If you need assistance in locating space to house your guests, contact your local Convention and Visitors Bureau (CVB). CVBs can help you locate hotels that have space for guests or a room for your party that meets your budget requirements. This will save you a lot of leg work, particularly if you live in one state and plan to marry in another.

Once you've located a hotel, it is a simple matter to reserve a block of rooms. Ask the hotel reservation department to set aside a block of rooms for your out-of-town guests. If the group is large enough, you may be able to get the rooms at a discounted price. It doesn't hurt to ask.

Ask the hotel to supply you with reservation cards that can be slipped into the mail with your wedding invitations. Some hotels have special ones that are just the right size to fit inside the invitation envelope. Others may only be able to supply you with a brochure that has the hotel's reservation number on it. Guests can check off the type of room they need, their arrival time, and method of payment.

When setting aside a block of rooms, ask the hotel to keep all the rooms in one area, for the convenience of your guests. You might also want to set up one room as a hospitality suite where your guests can gather. Mothers with young children may find the hospitality suite a convenient place to retreat to when the little ones get tired and fussy.

Before signing a contract with the hotel, be sure it specifies the following:

1. Check-in time. If the check-in time for your group is different from the norm, or if the time conflicts with the arrival and departure of another group, be sure to make arrangements ahead of time.

2. Check-out time and luggage storage. These normally apply to large groups such as conventions, but it doesn't hurt to check the hotel's rules. If normal check-out time is noon, and your guests will not depart until 2:00 p.m., make sure the hotel provides a secure place to store their luggage until it is time for them to leave.

3. Transportation. Does the hotel regularly run a shuttle bus to and from the airport, bus, or train station? If not, make arrangements for your guests to be transported to the hotel when they arrive.

4. Reservations. How will your group make reservations, and how will they pay? If your wedding weekend will take place at a resort and guests decide they like the atmosphere and wish to stay on longer, can they extend their stay at the same discounted room rate?

5. Release or cutoff date. By what date do you have to guarantee the rooms before they are released for general sale? What costs are involved if the guaranteed rooms are not used or if additional rooms are needed after the cutoff date?

One advantage of a B&B is that you can rent the entire house for your guests. B&Bs are perfect for small or second weddings. You can hold your rehearsal dinner there Friday evening, have a Saturday afternoon wedding and reception, and get up Sunday morning to a gift-opening party and breakfast. Look for B&B's that specialize in weddings and meetings. They'll be the ones best equipped to accommodate your group and will have the proper food and liquor licenses. Avoid those that cater to travelers only. Your local convention and visitors bureau should be able to help you locate the perfect B&B for your guests.

Your CVB can help in other ways, too. For instance, the CVB should be able to provide brochures or visitors' guides that list not only hotels, but restaurants and sight-seeing attractions as well. This guide should help your guests find entertainment when they're not involved in wedding activities.

The CVB can also help you organize your wedding-related

parties. For instance, it may be able to provide you with lists of caterers and decorating companies as well as ideas for unusual party sites. If your guests want to attend church or synagogue while they're in your city, a list of local churches or synagogues might also be available. (Such directories are usually found in hotel lobbies.)

Help your visitors get around town by providing maps of the area. Your convention and visitors bureau should have a supply on hand. Your CVB should also be able to give you telephone numbers for taxi and limousine service, rental car companies, bus transportation and trains and airlines serving your area.

If you'd like to give your out-of-town guests a guided tour of your city, your convention and visitors bureau can also help you locate tour companies.

Although their services are well-known to professional meeting planners, convention and visitors bureaus are an underused resource. Give your local representative a call when you're looking for ways of taking care of your out-of-town guests.

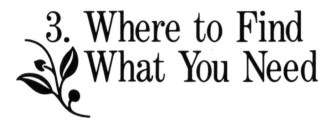

3. Where to Find What You Need

*T*he increase in the number of party supply stores has made party planning easier. You can walk into such shops and find decorations, gift-wrapping supplies, napkins, paper plates, and plastic utensils for almost any occasion you can think of. Many kinds of preprinted form invitations are available now, too — including those for engagement parties, bridesmaids' luncheons, and rehearsal dinners.

In many large cities, a new kind of publication is finding its way onto bookshelves in local libraries, bookstores, and newsstands. Called a party guide, party directory, or special-events planning guide, this type of book lists ideas and nearby resources for all kinds of parties. These listings are usually accompanied by a brief description of the services offered. Some books even contain coupons for discounts on services such as singing telegrams or hayrides, or products such as buttons, T-shirts, and the like. An invaluable tool, a party guide can save you time and leg work — a boon when you're planning an event as special as a wedding.

If you can't find a party guide in your area, the Yellow Pages will become your best resource. Let the headings be your guide: You should be able to find musicians under "Musicians." Sometimes the item or service you're looking for can be found in more than one place. For example, jukeboxes may be listed not only under "Jukeboxes," but also under "Party Supplies."

Often an item is not listed where you think it should be. Play the detective and follow your hunches. For example, "Uniforms" may not yield the cheerleaders' pom-poms you're searching for, while "Dance Supplies" may be a rich source of materials.

Your local library may have sources you might not have thought of. Libraries are also great places to find sheet music and records and tapes of folk and classical music, and other types of music you might not have in your personal collection. Don't hesitate to ask the librarians for help; they thrive on questions.

City and state tourism departments and convention and visitors bureaus can also be quite helpful in finding services and locations for parties. If you're planning a full-blown weekend wedding, ask them for literature on things to see and do in your area. (It might be a good idea to include this information with the wedding invitations you send to out-of-town guests.)

Last, don't be afraid to ask your friends for advice or recommendations.

To make your search easier, here is a general guide to finding some of the props, gifts, and favors mentioned in the party theme chapters of this book.

Airplane hangar . . . as in "Aviator's Rehearsal Dinner." Chances are, if you're going to use this theme, someone in your wedding party is already involved in aviation. This will give you a head start in locating a hangar in which to hold the party. (It's no problem at all, of course, if you own your own plane or are a member of a flying club.)

If the theme intrigues you and you don't have immediate access to a hangar, start your search by cruising through the Yellow Pages. Under "Aircraft" you'll find air charter operators and flight instruction schools. Although most of these places may be unwilling to rent out a hangar for a party (insurance costs in aviation are sky-high!), people in the business form a close-knit community. They know each other's business very well and are well acquainted with privately owned aircraft hangars around the airport. They can steer you to someone who will rent a hangar for such an important occasion. If at first you don't succeed, don't get discouraged. Hangars have been used for wedding receptions — much larger gatherings than your rehearsal dinner!

Baseball bases . . . as in "Saturday Softball Tournament." You should be able to find an inexpensive set of rubber bases at any sporting goods store. They're cheaper than the cloth bases used in regular softball tournaments and they're easier to paint on.

Beach balls and sand toys . . . as in "Summer Olympics Engagement Announcement" and "Midwinter Beach Party." Visit a toy store or the toy department of a discount store.

Bird bath . . . as in "Cupid's Temple of Love." Inexpensive plasticbird baths can be found at garden supply and hardware stores. If you'd like something a little more elegant, you can rent a fountain from a party supply company. Look for "Party Supplies" in the Yellow Pages.

Boats . . . as in "Rollin' on the River." Excursion and boat charter companies advertise frequently in newspapers, particularly during the summer months. Check the ads in the travel section of your local newspaper or look in the Yellow Pages under "Boat–Excursion" or "Boat–Charter."

Cheerleaders' pom-poms . . . as in "Saturday Softball Tournament." Try local theatrical supply stores, costume rental agencies, and companies that specialize in supplying dance costumes, shoes, and accessories. You may also want to try children's toy stores; they sometimes carry pom-poms as play items.

Chocolate roses . . . as in "Chocolataire." A candy store that specializes in gourmet chocolates is the place to visit. This is also the place you can find chocolate baskets, chocolate swans and **foil-covered chocolate coins** . . . as in "Pirate's Beach Party."

Disc jockey . . . as in "Back-to-the-Fifties Sock Hop." D.J.s abound. They're usually cheaper than live bands. Almost all of them come with their own light shows as well as a wide selection of music. In fact, the more lights, the better. Pick one that will play requests as well as concentrating on the "era" of your party. Locate them under "Disc Jockeys" in the Yellow Pages or through an entertainment agency.

Fabric paint . . . as in "Romantic Evening Shower" and "Library Shower." Tubes of fabric paint in a rainbow of colors can be purchased at fabric stores, hobby and craft shops, and discount stores. The paints also come in a variety of finishes such as puffy, glitter, shiny, and opalescent. Some fabric paints even change color with a change in temperature!

Foam core . . . as in "Cupid's Temple of Love." Foam core boards are often used to provide a stiff backing for mounting posters and large photos. Selected art supply stores and hobby and craft stores carry foam core in large sheets which you can cut to the length you need. Camera dealers and stores that sell photography and darkroom supplies may also have foam core on hand.

Gaming tables . . . as in "Casino Night." Firms that rent party supplies can help you out here. Some specialize in casino games and will even supply you with dealers if you need them. Find them in the Yellow Pages under "Party Supplies" and "Games."

Golf balls and tees . . . as in "Mixed-Doubles Golf Tournament." The Yellow Pages are full of companies that sell advertising specialties — everything from matchbooks to keychains. Concentrate on those that sell imprinted balloons and novelties rather than those that deal in large corporate incentive programs. You'll get better service, and they won't mind selling items to you in small quantities (although you may have to purchase twelve dozen golf balls!)

Helium balloons . . . as in "Sunday Send-Off" and "Post-Wedding Talent Show." Look under "Party Supplies" or "Balloons" in the Yellow Pages.

Hot air balloons . . . as in "Sunday Send-Off." Look under "Balloons–Hot Air" in the Yellow Pages. Flights with a celebratory bottle of champagne afterward are common. Some offer hors d'ouevres, chauffeur service, and video camera rental so you can tape the flight. Others advertise in-flight weddings. Nearly all have gift certificates available.

Jukebox . . . as in "Back-to-the-Fifties Sock Hop." Entertainment and party guides frequently list jukebox rental firms. If your community doesn't have such a book, check the Yellow Pages under "Jukeboxes" or "Party Supplies."

Magician and jugglers . . . as in "Camelot." This is where an entertainment or party guide comes in handy. However, the Yellow Pages can once again come to your rescue.

Professional magicians can be found, quite logically, under "Magicians." You can also locate them through magic and costume stores. When seeking a magician, be sure to specify that you are looking for someone who specializes in entertaining adults, rather than children.

Jugglers are a little trickier. Check local talent agencies for jugglers who may be listed with them, or look under "Juggling Supplies" in the Yellow Pages. Shops that sell balls and clubs to jugglers know their clientele well and should be able to steer you toward someone who entertains.

Miniature bride and groom . . . as in "Trim-the-Tree Announcement Party." These traditional cake decorations are easily obtained from bakeries, party supply stores, stationery stores . . . almost anywhere you find bridal accessories such as cake knives and champagne toast glasses.

Miniature shopping bags . . . as in "Treasure Hunt," and "Magical Mystery Tour." These are widely available in party supply stores, party sections of discount stores, and stationery stores.

Mini-pumpkins . . . as in "Halloween Shower." Your local farmer's market is the best place to purchase these harvest time gourds. Florist shops are another source, although slightly more expensive. Closer to Halloween, you may be able to find mini-pumpkins in supermarkets.

Mirror ball . . . as in "Prom Night." Look under "Party Supplies" in the Yellow Pages for companies that rent everything from tables and chairs to champagne fountains and dance floors.

Monofilament fishing line . . . as in "Fishing Frolic," "Look to the Future," and "Slippin' and Slidin' Party." You can find small reels of fishing line in hobby and craft stores; however, it's less expensive when purchased at a sporting goods store. Sporting goods stores also carry a wide array of fishing lures (as in "Fishing Frolic"). Some also have wildlife prints and sculptures (as in "Wild Game Rehearsal Dinner.")

Old-time photography . . . as in "Great Gatsby Photographer's Studio." The Yellow Pages are full of portrait photographers. What you're looking for is a portrait photographer who specializes in Victorian photography. Regions with a large tourist trade often have old-time photographers. While some photographers require patrons to come to their studios, others bring their equipment to the party site. (Still others rent their studios for an evening.) A Victorian photographer should have a full range of costumes, custom scenes, cutout boards, and other props designed to give instant sepia-toned photos an antique look.

Parchment paper . . . as in "Pirate's Beach Party." Parchment can be found in hobby and craft stores, art supply stores, and sometimes in stationery stores . . . wherever calligraphy supplies are sold.

Piñatas . . . as in "Friday Night Fiesta." These are widely available at party supply stores and in the party supply departments of discount stores. Stuff a piñata with wrapped candies and little plastic toys and you're all set.

Postcards . . . as in "Sunday Send-Off" and "Boys' Toys Shower." Prestamped postcards are as close as your local post office.

Printed napkins . . . as in "Barbecue Shower" and "Surprise-Announcement Party." Many printers who print wedding invitations also print napkins for wedding receptions. Look for those who specialize in letterpress printing. Letterpress is the old-fashioned way to print — straight from handset metal type or dies. Because they tear easily, napkins must be printed slowly; high-speed offset presses cannot be used. The ink is stamped onto the paper.

Lettering can be printed in foil inks in a process called gold-stamping, or with varnish inks. Be sure to give the printer plenty of time to print the invitations, since each napkin must be hand-fed into the press.

Psychics and tarot card readers . . . as in "Look to the Future." You won't find these people in the Yellow Pages. If you don't have a party or entertainment guide to consult, check for bookstores that specialize in the occult. Dealers there will know psychics and tarot card readers who frequent their stores and should be able to direct you to someone who entertains at parties.

Pumpkin lights . . . as in "Halloween Shower." Strings of pumpkin lights; windsocks in the form of ghosts, witches, and skeletons; and numerous other forms of Halloween paraphernalia can be found in card shops, drug stores, and novelty stores.

Seed corn caps . . . as in "Down-Home Rehearsal Dinner." If you live in a rural area, finding supplies for this type of party is easy. Visit your local grain elevator or feed mill and purchase the number of caps you need for your party. If you're a city dweller, don't despair. You can get what you need by calling Swingster Marketing's customer service department. The company has many seed corn companies as its clients and will sell caps in quantities as small as one dozen. The toll-free number is (800)848-8084. Explain to the customer service representative that you're having a party and would like to order caps as favors. The most readily available brands are DeKalb, Cargill Seeds, Funk's G, and Jacques (pronounced "Jakes.")

Square dance caller . . . as in "Down-Home Rehearsal Dinner" and "New Neighbors Welcome Party." If they're not listed in your phone book, you should be able to find callers through the Western apparel shops in your area. Since they provide costumes for square dancers, you should be able to find out the addresses of clubs in your area, and through the clubs, a caller. If all else fails, contact Callerlab, International Association of Square Dance Callers, Pocono Pines, PA 18350, (717) 646-8411. Callers should come equipped with their own music and sound systems.

T-shirts . . . as in "Groom's Bicycle Marathon" and "Saturday Softball Tournament." T-shirt shops that make up special shirts in quantities from one to infinity are everywhere. Chances are, there's one in your local shopping center or mall. If not, look under "T-shirts" in the Yellow Pages.

You can also make your own T-shirts. Hobby and craft stores carry fabric paint, dyes, and iron-on transfers to help you create unique designs.

Tents . . . as in "Presents in the Park." Shelter your guests from the elements by providing a tent. Companies that rent party supplies usually include tents and canopies in their inventories. Find them under "Party Supplies" or "Tents–Renting" in the Yellow Pages.

Travel posters . . . as in "Heritage Rehearsal Dinner," "Friday Night Fiesta," and "Sunday Send-Off." If your theme is strictly local, contact your city's convention and visitor's bureau. These bureaus sometimes send out posters to promote tourism. State tourism departments are another good source. There may even be a company in your area that specializes in selling travel posters and maps.

If your theme features another country, call a local travel agent and ask if he or she can provide you with the telephone number of the tourist board for the country you are interested in.

Most of these tourist offices charge a fee for the posters. It may be a flat fee or a sliding scale, depending on the quantity that you order.

Tour arrangers . . . as in "Wedding Weekend Sightseeing Tour." Out-of-town guests will appreciate a guided tour of your city. Contact your local convention and visitors bureau for names, addresses, and phone numbers of tour operators in your area.

"While You Were Out" Message Forms . . . as in "Home Office Shower." These come in many sizes and colors and are easily obtained at an office supply store. You should also be able to find envelopes that fit your memo invitation.

Many office supply centers also carry a wide range of small items that can be used as party favors, such as letter openers, erasers in novelty shapes, and giant paper clips.

Happy hunting!

4. Engagement Parties

*A*nnouncing an engagement used to follow a certain protocol: You told the woman's parents first. Then you told the man's family. Next, the bride's family announced the engagement publicly in the newspaper. Then, the groom's family held a party for the bride. Today, many couples prefer to host the announcement party themselves.

An Intimate Affair _____

Mom and Dad should certainly be among the first to know of your plans to marry. So should Grandma and your favorite Aunt

Helen. Dining *en famille* is a cozy, comfortable way to break the news. You and your beloved will be surrounded by the people you know best and love most.

Plan an intimate sit-down dinner for your closest family members in your home or apartment. The affair can be casual or formal, depending on your family's style. Because you're apt to be a bit excited, try to prepare some of the food ahead of time. Serve a simple but elegant meal: crown roast of pork, new potatoes in butter and chives, orange-glazed carrots, a spinach-and-onion salad. A good wine can make the meal complete. A simple bouquet of daisies or carnations is all that's needed to grace the table.

Just before you serve dessert (apples sprinkled with cinnamon, sugar, and nutmeg and baked in brandy or rum), tell your parents your good news. If the dinner is for his family, the groom should make the announcement. If it's for your family, you do the telling. Take a deep breath and begin: "Mom, Dad, Jim and I have talked it over, and we've decided to marry. We're very happy, and we'd like you to celebrate with us." Then open the champagne, and let the spirits flow!

Now's the time for a toast from the head of the family. He or she starts by saying, "I'd like to propose a toast." Everyone (except the bride and groom) rises, as Mom or Dad continues, "I've watched Sally (or Jim, if it's the groom's family) grow up. I've seen her (him) recover from scraped knees and broken hearts. She (he) has grown into a beautiful person, and a responsible adult. I've known Jim (Sally) for only a short while, but I know he's (she's) the kind of person I'd like to see my daughter (son) marry. I'm proud to welcome him (her) into our family."

After everyone has taken a sip of wine, the groom rises and briefly thanks the speaker: "Thank you for your kind words. You've always made me feel welcome, and I look forward to becoming a member of your family."

Rest assured that the evening will fly by as the conversation inevitably turns to discussion of the wedding date and any plans you may have made regarding your ceremony or honeymoon. Now's a good time to ask Grandma if she has anything "old," such as a lace handkerchief, that you can carry with you as you walk down the aisle.

Summer Olympics Engagement Announcement ___

The long, sunny days of summer were made for hosting athletic competitions. Take advantage of the good weather and use your family's lakeside cabin, mountain chalet, or oceanside cottage as the setting for your engagement announcement.

Invite family members and close friends to attend a picnic. Using a felt-tip pen, write the invitations on small, uninflated beach balls or children's toy life preservers, giving the time, date and location on one side. Allow the ink to dry, then draw a map showing the location of the party on the other side. Make sure the ink is completely dry on both sides of the invitation. Then fold each one carefully and place it in a 9″ x 12″ manila envelope for mailing. Guests will get the "big picture" when they inflate the ball or ring.

Throughout the day, hold Olympic-style contests. Water sports such as sailing, water-skiing, and swimming lend themselves naturally to good-natured competition. Or hold a softball tournament. You may even want to hold sack races. Give funny, homemade trophies to the winners. Add a dash of upbeat, popular music to the fun.

The picnic menu can include potato salad, baked beans, corn on the cob, grilled hamburgers on toasted buns, cold drinks, and fresh, juicy watermelon. A bright paper tablecloth and contrasting napkins and paper plates will make your wooden picnic table much more festive.

When everyone has gathered for the meal, tap a keg of beer, and make the big announcement. Bask in the warmth and good cheer of everyone's congratulations and good wishes, but be ready for some horseplay: Someone might decide to dunk the two of you in the water!

Prom Night

The senior prom is often one of life's most elegant affairs. Girls in satin and taffeta float down the stairs to meet self-conscious boys in rented tuxes. Starry-eyed couples walk arm-in-arm as they promenade around the ballroom. And who can forget the embarrassment of pinning a corsage for the first time? Relive those more innocent times on the night you announce your engagement to the world.

Invite both families and your friends to a private dinner dance. Ask them to dress in formal, "prom" attire. (You may even want to ask the women to wear the dresses they wore to their own proms!) Corsages and boutonnieres are *de rigueur* at this event.

(If a dinner dance is beyond your budget, you can make the party less expensive by serving refreshments and hors d'ouevres.)

Many proms have a theme such as "Gone with a Smile," or "A Night to Remember." Decorate the party room according to the theme you choose.

For your "prom night," you might want an upbeat theme like "All That Jazz." Decorations can be musical notes cut from cardboard and covered with foil. Suspend the notes from the ceiling with monofilament fishing line. Use the silvery notes on a backdrop behind the band. Foil-covered cutouts of saxophones, trumpets and clarinets would complete the scene. And don't forget to put notes on the backs of the music stands.

"Enchantment Under the Sea" is another good party theme. Decorate the room with painted cardboard fish, seashells, and an octopus or two. Paint a canvas backdrop of seaweed and coral for the band. If you will be serving dinner, place seashells painted with your name and the name of your fiancé at each place setting.

Whatever your theme, don't forget to hang a mirror ball in the center of the room to catch the light and send it spinning around the room.

Hire a photographer to snap a portrait of each couple. If some of your friends come to the party unescorted, have the photographer snap informal group pictures of them during the dance. The photographer should collect your friends' names and addresses so photos can be sent to them after the event.

When the moment's right, and with a flourish from the band, have a parent or an old friend make a formal announcement of your engagement: "Ladies and gentlemen, may I have your attention, please? We've all had a lot of fun tonight. And now I want to let you in on a little secret: This hasn't been a prom at all. It's an engagement party for Drew and Tammy, who have announced their intentions to be married next May. Congratulations and best wishes to you both!"

Back-to-the-Fifties Sock Hop

Your guests will "rock around the clock" at this 1950s engagement party.

Cut round invitations that look like 45-rpm records from black construction paper. Use white ink (available from art supply stores) to make the record label, telling the particulars of the party (reason, place, date, and time). Ask your friends to dress up in Fifties attire — poodle skirts, bowling shirts, blue jeans with rolled-up cuffs, and bobby socks and saddle shoes.

Rent a large space with plenty of dancing room; a school gymnasium or your apartment complex party room would be perfect. Or clear the clutter out of your parents' basement to make room to boogie. Decorate the room with colorful streamers and some pep rally signs like "Go, team, go!"

Rent a jukebox or hire a disc jockey to spin some favorite platters from the Fifties. You may want to stage a hula hoop contest, awarding a prize to the person with the "best wiggle." Give prizes for the best Fifties costumes, too. Or how about a limbo contest? The person who squeezes under the bamboo pole when it's just inches from the floor is the winner.

For refreshments, serve cherry colas. The authentic classic Coke® glasses are collectors' items, but you may be able to find plastic glasses that resemble the originals. Popcorn and potato chips make good, crunchy accompaniments.

Midway through the evening, have the disc jockey play a medley of first lines from Fifties tunes that describe your courtship or how you met (such as "Standing on the corner, watching all the girls go by"). As the medley winds down, have the D.J. make the announcement. "Jeff and Jody asked me to play that medley because it tells a little story about them. Now I think we should give them a round of applause — to congratulate them on their upcoming marriage!"

Let the good times roll!

Look to the Future

Offer your friends a glimpse of the future when you announce your engagement. Hire a psychic or tarot card reader to tell your guests' fortunes.

Design your invitations on plain white fold-over cards. On the cover, draw a crystal ball (if you're not very artistic, a circle balanced on top of a triangle will do). Underneath, write, "A Party Is in Your Future." Inside, write, "We intend to spend our future together. Come help us celebrate our engagement!" Give the date, place, and time, and note that a fortuneteller will make an appearance at the party.

Decorate a corner of your home or apartment as a "reading room" where consultations can take place. Enclose the space with some colorful fabric curtains or strings of beads. Use a bright paisley fabric for a tablecloth. With fishing line, hang aluminum foil stars and moons at various heights around the room. For an extra-mysterious effect, cover the windows with black plastic (available in long rolls from a garden supply or hardware store), and stick silvery moons, stars, and the signs of the zodiac to the plastic.

Obtain some gypsy violin music from your local library, and play it softly in the background. Keep the lighting low to heighten the mood. Burn incense or simmer some potpourri to add still more ambiance.

For appetizers, serve assorted cheeses and hot, spicy meatballs. Or fill your guests' stomachs with a soul-satisfying Hungarian goulash and crusty garlic bread, hot from the oven. Serve red wine from straw-wrapped bottles.

Give guests some time to loosen up and mingle. Then have the psychic or card reader arrive about an hour after the party begins. Guests can take turns consulting with the psychic while the others chat and enjoy the party.

It all bodes well for a good time!

Getting-to-Know-You Tea Service

Marriage joins not only a man and woman, but their families as well. At some point between your engagement and the wedding day, your family must meet his.

One grandmother volunteered her home as the gathering place. Using her best china and silver tea service, she served an elegant buffet of tea sandwiches, mints, nuts, punch, and coffee. Your grandmother may be delighted to host a similar party for you.

To make the most of an occasion such as this, have both sets of parents bring the family photo albums so you can share pictures of your growing-up years.

A family tree can be very helpful when you are introducing families. Instead of the familiar, chart-on-the-wall type, cut a branch from a real tree. Hang photos of the grandparents near the bottom of the tree. Use a separate branch for each group of cousins, aunts, and uncles. It's a very graphic way to show relationships and serves as a quick reminder when Great-aunt

Agnes momentarily forgets the name of someone she met five minutes ago.

To make introductions easier at a particularly large gathering, try the technique used by one family. Print name tags that state each person's relationship to the bride or groom such as, "Connie, cousin of the bride," or "Bob, brother of the groom."

At the appropriate moment, the bridal couple should be treated to a champagne toast. This can be done after all the introductions are made, before the buffet line is opened, or before dessert is served.

What a wonderful way to start a new branch of the family!

Trim-the-Tree Announcement Party

Christmas is a warm and loving time of year, a time when family members come home for the holidays and friends gather together. Small wonder that many couples choose to announce their engagement around Christmas. The warmth of the season makes your good news seem all the better.

Invite a few close friends over for a Christmas tree trimming party. For invitations, cut circles from red and green construction paper to resemble tree ornaments. Or cut out pine tree shapes. They don't have to be perfectly symmetrical to look good. However, if you're truly inept in the art department, a triangle balanced on a square will do just fine. On one side, write the date, place, and time of the party. Trim the other side of the invitation with glitter, rickrack, or sequins.

Fill a wassail bowl with hot, mulled cider or brandied egg nog. Set the bowl in the middle of a table draped with a red or green tablecloth and surround it with sprigs of holly. Place large bouquets of statice that has been dyed bright red and green and sprayed with glitter in vases and set them on the floor. Pop some popcorn. Set out trays of decorated Christmas cookies. Set a holiday mood by playing Christmas carols on the stereo. Light some pine- or cinnamon-scented candles.

To make the occasion extra-special, wrap some small Christmas ornaments and place them in a small pile under the Christmas tree. Guests may each choose one to take home to place on their own trees as a remembrance of your party.

Have some of your friends string the lights around the tree, while others link strands of popcorn and cranberries. Others can decorate the fireplace mantel with garlands of pine boughs or sprays of holly. Hang ribbon-wrapped sprigs of mistletoe in every doorway in the house. Save the tree's crowning glory until last. This year, do something different: Top your tree with a miniature bride and groom (available from most bakeries). Then make the big announcement: "I'm replacing my Christmas angel with a pair of angels this year. The one in white is me. The one in the tuxedo is Don. We're engaged!"

If your courtship has been a long one, don't be too surprised to hear your friends sing the "Hallelujah Chorus!"

New Year's Announcement Party

The beginning of a new year is a fine time to take stock of how far you've come and where you're going. This year, welcome the New Year with bells, laughter, and exciting news. Proclaim your love for all the world to hear.

Invite friends and relatives to attend an elegant black-and-silver dinner party. Cut stars from heavy white construction paper. Write the invitation on one side and cover the other side with silver glitter. Guests should come dressed in black or white, or — for the truly daring — silver.

As guests arrive at the party, give them each a black or silver mask to wear during the masquerade ball, which will begin after dinner.

Have strolling musicians or a three-piece ensemble play light music during dinner. Serve a catered sit-down dinner using the caterer's china and silver. To be truly elegant, have it served by waiters in "black tie" wear.

Place 3½" x 5" cards next to each guest's place at the table. Guests should write their New Year's resolutions on the cards and drop them into an old top hat. (If you don't have one, buy a paper hat from a party supply store.) The bride and groom should write their marriage resolutions on colored cards, so they look different from the others.

A few minutes before midnight, a designated person, perhaps the father of the bride (or her brother) dresses up as Father Time. This person draws the New Year's resolutions from the hat and reads them aloud. The resolutions of the bride and groom are read last. They should read something like this, "Dennis resolves to marry Lisa next September," or "Lisa resolves to spend the rest of her life with Dennis."

As the clock strikes midnight, pop the cork on a bottle of champagne. Hug your friends as they sing "Auld Lang Syne" and crowd around you to offer their congratulations and exclaim over your engagement ring.

When the ruckus dies down, play a little New Year's game. In an area where there is little danger of starting a fire, place a dozen candles in a row and light them. The candles should be one foot apart from each other. Ask guests to jump the candles one at a time. The first candle extinguished indicates the month in which the jumper will marry. If none of the candles goes out, that person will not marry during the coming year.

When the party's over and everyone's gone home, prepare yourself — and your betrothed — for a New Year's kiss you'll never forget.

Midwinter Beach Party _____

If it's been a long, cold winter, your friends will surely remember your engagement party if you take them to the beach. Better yet, bring the beach to them.

Arrange to use the pool at a local hotel. Have the hotel staff set up patio tables with umbrellas and lounge chairs. If the hotel doesn't have them, perhaps you can bring in some of your own. Scatter a few beach balls around the pool perimeter.

For invitations, put a little sand into a self-sealing sandwich bag. Then staple each "beach in a bag" to a brightly colored note card. Tell your guests to wear their summer clothes — shorts, T-shirts, sundresses, sandals — and remind them to bring their bathing suits for a dip in the pool.

For refreshments, ask the hotel to provide a ten-gallon container of cold lemonade and let the guests serve themselves. Or provide a cash bar. (Of course, you'll pay for the champagne to be used later for the toast.) A buffet of summer foods such as hot dogs, barbecued ribs, and potato salad should be offered.

Use children's beach toys for table centerpieces. Fill toy buckets with a small amount of sand. Stick two miniature shovels labeled with the names of the bride and groom in each bucket.

Stretch a net across one end of the pool and play a rousing game of water volleyball with the bride as captain of one team and the groom as captain of the other. After the game, announce that the two of you will be playing as a "team" from now on.

Then pour the champagne, slip some Beach Boys music into the cassette player, and have fun, fun, fun!

Cupid's Temple of Love _____

What day could be more romantic to announce your engagement than St. Valentine's Day?

Invite your friends and relatives to a Valentine's Day party by mailing out — what else? — valentines! Make your own from red construction paper cut into double heart shapes. Decorate the valentines with doilies, glitter, and whatever else strikes your fancy. On the inside write "Cupid's darts have pierced our hearts. Join us as we celebrate our engagement!" Give the date, place, and time of the party. Just for fun, ask your guests to bring enough homemade valentines to exchange among themselves (be sure to tell them how many people you've invited!)

Decorate your living room to look like a Roman temple. Place a piano bench or chaise longue in one corner and drape it with a plain colored sheet; red, pink, or white would work best. Drape a couple more sheets across the tops of the windows like valences or swags. Tie the center and sides of the valence top together with red ribbons.

If you can, flank your entryway with a pair of wooden pillars topped with potted Boston ferns. You may be able to buy some pillars from an architectural salvage dealer who salvages pieces of old houses and sells them to people who are renovating their homes. If purchasing a pair is beyond your budget, try renting them from the prop department of a theatre or from a photography studio. Or build some out of sheets of foam core. It is inexpensive and lightweight, yet strong enough to hold up a potted plant. Cut the foam core to the length you want; then score it and roll it to make the sides. Set each pillar in a foam core base with a circle cut out of the center. Spray-paint the pillar or marbelize it with a sponge dipped in paint. If all else fails, draw pillars on long sheets of freezer paper. Hang the drawings on each side of your Roman bench, and place the ferns on the floor.

Light the room with as many candles as you can find. They needn't be expensive tapers. Plumbers' candles are available at most hardware stores. They burn a long time and are fairly inexpensive.

For music, obtain Mantovani records from your local library. The lush music of the violins will provide the right romantic atmosphere. Or play recordings by your favorite groups. Be sure to include your "special" song.

For a centerpiece, fashion a huge heart out of cardboard and cover it with red foil. Cut out a cardboard triangle, fold the sides toward the middle and glue the folded triangle to the back of the foil-covered heart. Stand the heart in the middle of the refreshment table. Cover the table with a solid-color cloth in red, pink, or white. Fill an inexpensive "silver" meat platter (available at most grocery stores) with heart-shaped cookies decorated with red sugar or pink icing. Set a glass bowl with chocolate bonbons near the centerpiece.

Buy an inexpensive plastic bird bath and fill it with a red punch "love potion." Stand the bird bath next to the refreshment table.

As they arrive at the party, have guests place their valentines in a box covered with hearts and cupids. Toward the end of the evening, have someone "play Cupid" and deliver the valentines to all the guests.

Who knows? Perhaps Cupid's arrows will pierce some of your friends' hearts, too!

5. Parties with Your Bridesmaids

*A*s the wedding day draws near, your days as a single woman are numbered. Take time to savor your friendships. Spend time doing things with "just us women." Think of special ways to tell your bridesmaids you appreciate them and thank them for being in your wedding.

Chocolataire

At the beginning of the 20th century, a new kind of party was in vogue — the Chocolataire. Everything on the menu for these afternoon or early evening dessert parties was made of chocolate: chocolate cake, chocolate ice cream, chocolate bonbons, even chocolate lemonade!

If your bridesmaids are confirmed chocoholics, treat them to an updated version of a Chocolataire. And let your sweet tooth run wild!

Cover the table with a lace tablecloth. Float a rose in a bowl of water. Write the name of each guest on a place card and tie each card to a long-stemmed chocolate rose (available at gourmet chocolate stores). Set each place with a dainty china demitasse cup. Each cup should be different. At the end of the feast, give each bridesmaid her cup and saucer as a thank-you gift.

Fill each cup with hot chocolate or chocolate-flavored coffee. (Offer tea or soft drinks for guests who don't care for coffee or chocolate.) Pile a tiered serving tray with white and dark chocolate truffles, fudge, and chocolate-covered cherries. Use a chocolate basket to serve strawberries dipped in chocolate, or melt chocolate in a fondue pot and let guests dip fresh pineapple, berries or marshmallows in the warm goo. (Guests who aren't fervently addicted to chocolate can snack on the fruit by itself.) For "dessert," serve chocolate cake, chocolate ice cream or a delicate chocolate mousse. Follow with an "after-dinner" drink of creme de cacao.

When everyone's craving for chocolate has been satisfied (if this doesn't do it, nothing will!), sit back and review your wedding schedule with your attendants. What a sweet way to spend an afternoon!

"Pink" Tea

"Pink" Teas were popular in the early 1900s. Unlike the Chocolataire, this social custom took its name not from the food, but from the table linens. Tablecloths, napkins, and china were all the same color. Although pink was the popular choice, blue, yellow, or green could also be used.

You can put on an inexpensive pink tea using paper table-cloths and napkins, plates, and cups. Use fresh flowers such as pink carnations or Sweetheart roses to decorate the table. If you have a solarium or greenhouse, place the tables and chairs among the ferns and other potted plants for a Victorian effect. Tie pink ribbons to the backs of the chairs.

Tea or coffee and shrimp salad are appropriate menu items. Or try dainty watercress-and-cream cheese sandwiches. Carry out your color scheme by serving raspberry sherbet or frozen strawberry yogurt for dessert.

Take this opportunity to present thank-you gifts to your bridesmaids. Frilly pink nightgowns or pink coral earrings make pleasing gifts.

If pink is not your cup of tea, use your favorite color or the wedding colors as the basic thematic element of this mini-celebration!

Cultural Tour

Meet your attendants at a local art or historical museum and spend a pleasant Saturday morning poking around the artifacts. If you've never been there before, ask a docent to give you a guided tour. Your group will pick up many tidbits of information they might otherwise miss.

Many museums have restaurants where you can retire for a lovely luncheon. Or perhaps there is a good restaurant nearby. Relax and discuss the Impressionists over a glass of white wine.

Express your appreciation to your attendants by giving them their thank-you gifts (something from the museum shop, perhaps?). If possible, make arrangements ahead of time to have the waiter bring the gifts to the table on a serving tray.

If you have time, return to the museum for a second look at some of your favorite exhibits. Or visit a wing you missed the first time around. Your guests will appreciate the quality time, and it will be a lovely "time out" from the busy whirl of wedding activities.

High Tea

A day spent touring the bridal shops searching for the right dresses can be a trying ordeal. Take a tip from the British and pop into the lobby of one of your area's more prestigious hotels for a spot of tea.

Many hotels in the United States now serve high tea in their lobbies, often to the accompaniment of soft piano music. You and your bridesmaids can relax in the elegant surroundings while you restore your energy.

Usually there is a basic per-person charge for this event, but guests may eat as much as they desire. Clotted cream and scones are often a high tea highlight. Count on going off your diet for the day.

While you're feeling veddy, veddy English, why not give your attendants a gift from the British Isles — a Waterford crystal pendant or tree ornament, perhaps.

As the tea and the music settle your jangled nerves, discuss the various dresses you've seen and tried with your attendants. Who knows? Perhaps the tea will help you come to a decision!

A Very Fitting Party

Make that last fitting at the bridal shop a real party. Have each attendant bring the undergarments and shoes she plans to wear in the wedding, and then have each one try on her gown. If the dresses fit as they should, all that's left are the rehearsal and the ceremony itself.

Take time now to thank your bridesmaids for their help by inviting them to a festive lunch in your home or at a good restaurant. Place small nosegays or tiny candles in holders at each place to brighten the table. If the party is at your home, scatter confetti and thin streamers across the tablecloth.

At home, serve fresh asparagus wrapped in Swiss cheese, ham and pastry. Offer fresh fruits for dessert. At the restaurant, allow each guest to order from the menu (you pick up the tab). Make arrangements ahead of time to have a specially decorated cake delivered to the table for dessert. Have the baker write "Thank You" across the cake with frosting, followed by the attendants' names.

As the lunch draws to an end, go around the table and thank each woman individually. As you do so, present her with a beautifully wrapped thank-you gift — a lapel pin to recall the pinning and fitting sessions, or a pair of earrings to match her gown. If you wish your attendants to wear special stockings (rhinestones up the back?), present these to them at this time.

Bridesmaids' Tanning Treat

One thoughtful attendant organized a party at a suntanning parlor. The bride was met at the door by her attendants, who wore sunglasses with the bride's name written on one lens, and the groom's name on the other.

Soft drinks and snacks were served as the bride opened envelopes containing certificates for services offered at the salon. Then the bride was treated to a manicure, pedicure, facial massage, body massage, full tanning — all gifts from her attendants. The organizer of the shower said the point of the party was "utter frivolity" and the gifts had "no long-term practical use whatsoever."

You can give your attendants a golden glow by treating each of them to a session in the tanning bed as a thank-you gift. Many tanning salons offer package rates. Buy a package and split the sessions among your bridesmaids. If, for health reasons, your attendants do not wish to use the tanning booth, offer them a certificate for a manicure instead.

A day or two ahead of the wedding, invite the bridesmaids to a party at the salon. Offer your attendants soft drinks, crackers and fresh fruits and vegetables to munch on as they wait their turn under the lights. Immerse yourselves in "girl talk" as you move into the final hours of your life as a single woman.

Bridesmaid Makeover Tips_____

You want everyone to look her best on your wedding day. Why not plan a get-together with your bridesmaids and invite a makeup expert to the party? The makeovers will be your thank-you gift to each attendant.

The expert can help each woman find the makeup most suited to her complexion, and can help choose colors that coordinate with the attendants' gowns. The expert can also provide tips on applying the makeup so that each bridesmaid will look elegant.

Provide some light refreshments and plenty of tissues and cold cream as the bridesmaids experiment with their new looks. Tip: Before the wedding, try on your veil or headpiece, and have the attendants try on their hats. You may need to make a slight change in your hair style to support your headpiece. Why not invite your hair stylist to the makeover party, too?

Magical Mystery Tour _____

One bride's friends treated her to a day-long "Magical Mystery Tour." The bride was told to meet her friends at a certain place at 7:00 a.m. She was to dress nicely and to be prepared to spend the entire day touring the city.

The bride and her attendants boarded a chartered bus and set out on their tour. At midmorning, they stopped for coffee. For lunch, they stopped at a quaint little café. At dinner, they ate in another elegant restaurant. In between, they toured dozens of shops and boutiques and did some sightseeing as well.

You could use this idea for a wedding shopping expedition with your attendants. Draw up some bus "tickets" or use actual tokens to invite the women on the tour. Have them meet you at an appointed place and time. Hire a van or limousine to chauffeur you from place to place. (This eliminates time lost searching for a parking place.) Be sure to include a stop for lunch.

At the conclusion of the tour, give each attendant a thank-you gift in a miniature shopping bag (you can buy these bags at party-supply stores). Appropriate gifts include a designer key ring, a handbag, or a gift certificate from one of the stores at which you shopped.

Bachelorette Boogie

While the groom is having his stag party, the bride and her attendants can have a night out on the town, too. You need not worry about thank-you gifts for this party; the bridesmaids are taking *you* out for a final fling.

Start out with drinks and a meal of hors d'ouevres at a favorite after-work gathering place. Talk about last-minute wedding preparations, your last fitting session, or the schedule for the wedding day as you nibble on Buffalo chicken wings and crudites and dip. Don't be surprised if your attendants urge you to try out a wild new drink combination or give you a last-minute shower of personal gifts such as perfume, chemises, or nightgowns.

When happy hour has ended, move on to a comedy club, where you can forget your cares and share some laughs (even better if it's an all-woman revue!).

End the evening by dancing away your wedding jitters at your favorite disco. When you return to your home, tired and happy, you'll be glad you had this "last chance" evening with your girlfriends.

6. Women-Only  Showers

Although couples showers are becoming more common, it's still fun for women to get together by themselves. But that doesn't mean the showers have to follow the same old formula. Break away from tired old games and have fun!

Romantic Evening Shower _____

A bride who's been treated to two or three showers and is up to her ears in towels and muffin pans will appreciate this variation of the familiar lingerie shower idea.

Using fabric paint, print the shower invitation on an embroidered linen handkerchief. The wording can be something like this: "Help Jan and Gene keep the fires of romance glowing by providing all the ingredients for a romantic evening." Give the date, place, and time of the shower.

Decorate the party room with hearts and cupids and pink and white streamers. Use a pink tablecloth on the buffet table, and place a huge bouquet of long-stemmed red roses in the center. Give a rose to each guest to take home. Pin a rose-and-lace corsage on the bride.

Serve frozen daiquiris and light hors d'ouevres if this is an after-work get together, or put together a salad and dessert bar for your guests.

Gifts can include theater tickets, a peignoir set, a bottle of wine, a pair of candles in pretty holders, or the bride's favorite perfume. If this is a second marriage and the pair has young children, a gift certificate for babysitting services would be most appreciated. The gifts should be accompanied by advice, both practical and funny, on how to keep the honeymoon going. The bride should read the suggestions aloud to the group.

Be sure to take lots of pictures to present to the bride as a keepsake.

Treasure Hunt

Though this shower takes a little advance planning, it should be fun for all involved.

Stuff a miniature shopping bag (available at party-supply stores) into the shower invitation, or write the invitation on the bag itself. In the invitation, direct your guests to purchase a gift for the bride, have it wrapped and leave it at the store. (To make things easier for the bride, have all the guests shop at the same store.)

Ask each guest to volunteer for a different department, such as lingerie, housewares, furniture, or china. The first to call in her R.S.V.P. gets first choice.

Write clues for the bride to follow. For example, a gift of lingerie could be clued by "Keep me close at night." An overnight bag might say "Please take me with you." Have all the guests meet at the wedding registration department. Different guests will then accompany the bride to each department listed in the clues. For example, one will accompany her to china, another to luggage, another to housewares. After each gift is found, the bride and the guests return to the registration department. The search ends when each guest has accompanied the bride around the store.

After the hunt, retire to a cozy little restaurant to meet the guests, open the gifts, and have lunch!

Bridal Quilting Bee _____

Handmade quilts, like oriental rugs, have a tendency to become valuable heirlooms as they age. Gather the nimble-fingered and create a heirloom bridal quilt, using the color scheme from the couple's future bedroom.

Cut the blocks ahead of time, and provide one to each guest as she joins the party. Experienced hands help the novices as everyone hand-appliqués a simple design to a background block. Have each quilter sign her name on her completed block with indelible ink. Or embroiderers in the group can stem-stitch over the signatures for a raised effect. To create a treasured heirloom, have your best embroiderer stitch the names of the couple and their wedding date on a block for the center of the quilt. As each block is completed, the quilters should hand it to the bride, who pins the blocks together for assembly on the sewing machine. When the quilt top is assembled, sew it to the back, fill it with polyester quilt batting, stitch it closed. Tie off individual squares with yarn.

Be sure to have plenty of light refreshments on hand. With a cooperative project such as this, conversation should flow easily as the work progresses.

At the end of the party, present the completed quilt to the bride. It's a gift she'll treasure, and she'll remember the givers each time she uses it.

Halloween Shower

Kids aren't the only ones who like to dress up on Halloween. One woman held a Halloween shower for a cousin who was to be married in November.

Black-and-orange invitations asked guests to come in costume. The bride, who was appropriately dressed as an angel, was asked to award a prize for the best costume. (She judiciously chose her grandmother.)

Guests also bobbed for apples suspended on a string from the ceiling and pinned the nose on the witch. You can also stage a pumpkin-carving or painting contest using mini-pumpkins.

A large pumpkin was hollowed out and used as a vase for a floral centerpiece. Guests' names were written on mini-pumpkins, which served as place cards. Strings of pumpkin-shaped lights, available at novelty and card shops, blinked in the windows.

Hot apple cider, coffee, and pumpkin pie were the refreshments at this evening party.

Mother-of-the-Bride Shower

Although the groom will provide his mother-in-law-to-be with a corsage on the wedding day, "Mom" may still be feeling somewhat left out during the hustle and bustle of the weeks and days preceding the ceremony. Why not give her a survival kit to help her make it through the big day?

Invite some of her intimate friends over for a Saturday luncheon. For invitations, fold a piece of colored paper in half. On the outside, draw a picture of a doctor's bag and label it

"Mom's Wedding Survival Kit." Inside, write, "Mary's not losing a daughter, she's gaining a son. Let's help her have some wedding fun." Explain that guests should bring gifts to help Mary "survive" the wedding; then give the date, place, and time for the shower.

Create a pleasant atmosphere by setting a simple but pretty table. Place some flowers in a shiny copper teakettle. Use plaid or checkered placemats and napkins.

Food can be simple. Chicken salad on melon wedges, dinner rolls, and a fluffy lemon mousse go together nicely. Add a bottle of good wine and some coffee with dessert, and your menu is complete.

Gifts can be funny, such as a lacy handkerchief and a bottle of aspirin, or thoughtful, such as a gift certificate for long-distance telephone calls (especially helpful if the bride is moving out of state).

Mom is sure to appreciate the gifts. Most of all, she'll welcome the time spent with her friends during this busy time of her life.

Supermarket Shower

We've all heard of grocery showers where the bride is given gifts of canned goods. One smart shower giver took the idea and gave it a unique twist that lifted the party into the "super" category.

Guests were invited to arrive at a local supermarket at 7:30 p.m. on a weeknight, when regular shopping traffic was light. (The hostess made arrangements ahead of time with the store manager.) Guests were to bring the cash they would have spent on a gift, and a small gift enclosure card.

Upon arrival, each guest received a corsage made from a white clothespin decorated with the bride's colors. The names of the bride and groom and the wedding date were written on streamers, which cascaded down from the corsage. The corsage was topped with a small plastic food product purchased at a toy store. Magnets were glued to the back of the corsage, which served double duty as a party favor and, later on, as a refrigerator magnet. The bride was given a larger corsage and an apron featuring her wedding color scheme. She wore the corsage and apron as she unloaded the shopping carts.

Grocery carts were decorated with posterboard signs that read "Grocery shopping is fun" and "Countdown, 11 days." Large bows were tied to the handles.

The bride was given a special chair — a bar stool — to sit on at the front of the store near the check-out lanes as her guests did the shopping. The stool was decorated with bows and a sign that read "I'm the Bride-to-Be."

Guests were divided into groups of three and four (to help them get acquainted with each other). From a decorated basket, each group drew a card bearing the number or description of a designated shopping aisle. The guests brought the filled carts to a specially designated check-out counter where the bride emptied out the contents and returned items she thought she might not use. Any money that was not used was given to the store manager, who wrote out a gift certificate to be used by the bride after her honeymoon.

When the shopping spree ended, guests took the bagged groceries to a nearby church fellowship hall, where refreshments were served. Because it was late by the time everyone shopped and returned to the church, guests were served cake, sherbet punch, mints, and nuts.

Guests had been asked to bring a favorite recipe on a recipe card. As a means of awarding door prizes, the bride-to-be drew these cards out of a decorated basket. Guests were also given envelopes for thank-you cards, which they addressed to themselves. The bride pulled one of these out of the basket for a final door prize.

Although the shower required a great deal of organization, all the guests had a good time. So did the supermarket manager!

7. Couples Showers

S	*howers needn't be only for the bride. More and more*
	couples today are being feted together. After all, it
takes two to make a marriage!

Gourmet Cooking Party —————

Sharing kitchen duties is becoming commonplace as more couples rely on two incomes. Cooking together is becoming one of life's great indoor pastimes. Couples who cook together like to mingle with other couples who cook, so why not throw a gourmet cooking party?

Invite three or four couples (or more, depending on the size of your kitchen) to attend by printing the invitation on the backs of potholders or in the bowls of large wooden spoons. Ask them to bring their favorite recipes and the necessary ingredients to prepare them in your kitchen. To avoid duplication, you may want to assign a salad to one couple, an entree to another, and a dessert to another.

Provide wines appropriate to each course, and sweeten the atmosphere with light classical music and bouquets of fresh flowers. This is an occasion that calls for your best crystal, china, and linens.

After the dinner, guests present the bridal couple with a copy of the recipe they prepared and a utensil needed to make the dish. (This could be as simple as a garlic press or something as gourmet as a pan for baking French bread.) The recipe cards are placed in a recipe file decorated for the occasion. A memorable way to recall a fine meal!

Be sure to take advantage of all the help in the kitchen by asking one couple to clear away the dinner dishes while another washes them and still another returns the china to the china cabinet. After cleanup is completed, let everyone settle back for an after-dinner glass of wine and some good conversation.

Stock-the-Wine-Cellars Shower

A couple that entertains frequently probably makes good use of a wine cellar or liquor cabinet. Stock their bar with a little help from friends.

To prepare invitations, soak the label from a wine bottle in water, then carefully remove the label so that it comes off in one piece. Allow it to dry flat on a piece of paper. Photocopy the label onto colored paper and use it as the cover for your invitations. Inside write, "It's a vintage year! Come to a couples shower for Joe and Sherry and help them stock their bar." Give the place, date, and time.

Ask the couples you invite to bring an assortment of wines, liquors, and drink mixes. Glassware — from shot glasses to pilsners to brandy snifters — and wine racks are also appropriate gifts. A bartender's guide to mixing drinks is another good gift idea.

Make the party a learning session by tasting different wines and cheeses. (Invite a local wine expert to the party to lead the group through the tasting.) Follow up with hot espresso and a delicious chocolate dessert.

Give each guest a parting gift: A box of cordial-filled chocolates.

Garden Party

A young couple who has just purchased a new home will need several items to help them maintain the exterior of their home. Although tea and scones could be served, this garden party is meant to provide the bridal couple with tools for doing yard work.

Hold the party outdoors. String Japanese lanterns among the trees, or place tiki torches around the perimeter of your deck or patio. Put a bright plastic tablecloth on the picnic table and use coordinating paper plates, cups, and flatware. Fire up the barbecue and serve up grilled chicken, crisp salads, and tall, cold drinks.

To make invitations, photocopy the front of a seed packet onto bright yellow paper and fold the paper in half. Under the picture, write, "You're invited to a Garden Party." Write the details inside — date, place, and time—, along with an explanation that guests should bring gifts to help the bridal couple with their yard work.

Gifts can include hedge clippers, line trimmers, spades, shovels, garden hoses, pruning shears, even a wheelbarrow or lawn mower. Don't forget to give a double hammock for relaxing in when all the work is done! If children are invited, they can get involved with the gift giving by presenting packets of seeds, garden gloves, or small potted outdoor plants. Other gift suggestions include equipment for yard games such as badminton, volleyball, or bocce ball.

As they work on their new landscape, the couple will appreciate the help you've given them by providing the appropriate tools for maintaining their little corner of the outdoors.

Four Seasons Shower _____

There's a "time for every matter under heaven," wrote the preacher in Ecclesiastes. To help the happy couple mark the seasons of their lives, give them gifts appropriate to each season of the year.

Tear pages from a pocket calendar to use as the cover for your invitation. Glue or paste the calendar page to a folded sheet of paper. On the inside, include the usual information such as date, location, and time of day.

Assign each pair of guests a season of the year and ask them to bring a gift appropriate for those months. For example, in winter, a couple might need an electric blanket or a snow shovel. In summer, a pair of beach towels might be perfect. A turkey platter would be appropriate for fall, and colorful umbrellas would come in handy during spring rains. Keep track of the assignments, and have the couple open the gifts in order as the year progresses.

To make the party even more fun, ask guests to come to the party dressed for the season to which they have been assigned. Guests can let their imaginations run wild with this idea — and they probably will!

(A variation on this theme takes the couple through the hours of the day: for example, an electric coffee grinder at 7:00 a.m.; a bottle of amaretto and a romantic videotape at 11:00 p.m. Guests could appear in anything from pajamas to business suits.)

For party favors, give your guests pocket calendars or date-books for the upcoming year. Be sure to mark the couple's wedding day or first anniversary in bright red letters.

Rest assured that this couples shower will be remembered — in whatever season it's held!

Western Shower

If the bridal couple are confirmed horse lovers, give them a Western shower. Even if they aren't, this party suggestion should prove fun. Make arrangements with a local riding stable to reserve a haywagon and party room.

Cut large horseshoes from gray paper and write the party details along the contours. Or cut small horseshoes from foil and glue them to a folded white card. Give the date, place, and time, and tell guests to come in Western gear — boots, bandannas, hats, prairie skirts, and blue jeans. Ask the stable to place a few old saddles, halters, and bridles around the room for decorations.

Put red-and-white checked cloths on the tables, and use folded red bandannas as napkins. Use tin pie plates to serve up the cowboy grub (chili and baking powder biscuits).

Play country and Western music on the jukebox, or bring in tapes featuring some of the old cowboy stars such as Gene Autry, Ernest Tubbs, and Hank Williams. Or have a guitarist in your group lead everyone in some rousing choruses of "Home on the Range" and "Whoopee Tie-Yi-Yo."

After the couple opens their gifts, head out to the barn for an old-fashioned hayride under the stars.

Library Shower

No home should be without a dictionary. And almost everyone needs a photo album or two. For a pair of bookworms, there's nothing nicer than a shower of books.

What better place to hold a book shower than in a room full of books? Many public libraries have meeting rooms available for rental on an hourly basis during regular library hours. Some may have restrictions on food or drink, and most will probably charge a fee for janitorial services. If that's too restrictive, you might try someone's home library or den. Or wheel a cartload of books into the family room.

Make invitations in the form of a book cover. If you're really creative, write a "novel" invitation — "Jane and John — Love Story of a Century." Or issue library cards stating the date, place, time, and purpose of the gathering.

During the shower, divide guests into groups of three and pass out pens and paper to every third person in the room. Ask this person to act as secretary for the group, which will create the couple's love story. Assign different parts of the story to each group — the couple's meeting, their first fight, and so on. The tale can be based on fact or can be totally fictional. After 10 minutes, collect all the stories and put them between the "cover." Ask the bride and groom to take turns reading "their" love story.

For refreshments, serve wine and cheese. Give bookmarks with the names on the bride and groom done in needlepoint or counted cross stitch as party favors. If needlework defies you, use fabric paint to write the names of the bride and groom on bookmarks made from strips of brightly colored felt.

Gifts for the couple can include not only books, but bookends and bookshelves. Gear the reading material to the couple's interests — sports, gardening, cookbooks, or mysteries, for example.

Dedicated book-lovers will appreciate the help you've given them in building their home library — every time they pick up a book!

Barbecue Shower

Bring the gang together on the deck or patio for this couples party.

Find a printer who specializes in printing napkins for wedding receptions, and have your shower invitations printed on napkins. Invitations could read, "Backyard barbecue shower for Jack and Linda. Help them cook up a storm!" Be sure to add the time, place, and date. On the bottom of the invitation, add "Please bring gifts for their barbecue" and give your phone number for calling in R. S. V. P.s. Supply an alternative date in case of rain the day of the shower.

Roast as many foods as possible on the grill — turkey legs, fruit kebabs, ears of corn, and so on. Gifts can be anything to do with barbecuing — a good basting brush, a chef's apron, a bag of charcoal briquettes.

If you have room, get up a friendly game of horseshoes. Throw in some country-Western music, and you've got a party!

Home Office Shower

Every home needs an office — a quiet place to pay the bills, keep household records, and compute income taxes. Help your bridal couple set up their own home office.

Send invitations on "While You Were Out" telephone message pads. Fill in the blanks: "Dick and Mary Harmon of (write in your address and phone), want to see you. Please call. Message: They are having a home office shower for Dale and Debbie on (date) at (time). Please bring gifts to help them set up an office at home." (See sample below.)

If you are inviting an after-work crowd, serve appetizers and cocktails. Or, if you have the time and ambition, put on a buffet dinner of quiche, stuffed mushrooms, muffins and a tossed salad. If you're holding the shower on a weeknight, be sure it breaks up early so everyone can get to bed early for work the next morning!

Appropriate gifts range from a roll of stamps in an attractive dispenser to floppy disks for the couple's personal computer. A tape dispenser, stapler, a bill organizer, a box of file folders, and a good pair of scissors are also handy gifts. Some couples may wish to share the cost of expensive gifts such as a two-drawer filing cabinet or a telephone answering machine.

While You Were Out

For _____ Date _____

Time _____ A.M. _____ P.M.

M _____

of _____

_____ phoned _____ returned your call

_____ please call _____ will call again

_____ came to see you _____ wants to see you

Phone _____
          area code   number   extension

Message
_____

_____

_____

_____

_____

_____

_____

"Storm"

One couple had been showered with nearly every conceivable type of gift. Their linen closets bulged with new sheets and towels. Their kitchen was equipped with the latest cookware. Still, the bride's sister wanted to do something special. Two weeks before the wedding, she invited the couple and their friends to a "storm" shower.

She asked guests to bring "different" spices and liqueurs — items a person wouldn't ordinarily buy for a kitchen or bar. Silly gifts were also welcome at this shower. The emphasis was on fun and novelty, rather than on expensive or practical gifts.

You can take this anti-shower theme further by inviting friends of the bridal couple to bring "white elephant" gifts to bestow upon the pair. The more useless the item, the better. It's a great way to clean out closets and have fun doing it. (At the end of the evening, the couple may want to turn the tables on the guests and give the gifts back!)

You can also ask guests to bring the worst photos they can find of the bride or groom. These can be presented in a framed collage, in a scrapbook for a keepsake, or in a pile, to be ceremoniously burned by the bride and groom!

8. Parties with Your Groomsmen

*G*irls popping out of cakes are passé. When today's groom goes out for a last fling with the guys, he's likely to be doing something more active.

Groom's Day at the Racetrack

Playing the ponies is all the more fun when it's done with friends. Take the groom out to the racetrack for a winning afternoon.

Horse racing is a sport that takes place in all kinds of weather, so be sure to dress appropriately. If you can, arrive at the track early enough to watch the horses go through their paces. Stroll through the stables and talk to the grooms and trainers. You may pick up some tips on the day's races. Arm yourselves with a supply of racing forms.

At lunch time, the guys should pitch in and buy the groom lunch as he studies the forms. Just for the fun of it, take up a collection and give the groom some extra cash to use at the tellers' windows. Place some wild bets amongst yourselves. With luck, everyone will come away with a few extra dollars in their pockets, and odds are good that everyone will have a good time.

Camping Weekend

Get away from the hustle and bustle of wedding preparations with a leisurely weekend of camping and canoeing. This guys-only outing is just what the doctor ordered to reduce pre-wedding tension. Consult with your state department of tourism to locate the perfect campsite for your expedition.

If sleeping out under the stars seems a little *too* rough, try a guided fishing trip. Many resorts provide a boat and motor, refreshments, and a shore lunch, as well as a knowledgeable, experienced guide to help you find those lunker bass or lake trout. They also have facilities for cleaning the fish and will store them in the freezer so you can take them home for dinner.

Because a canoe expedition or staying at a resort can be expensive, agree to share expenses for food, lodging, and transportation before setting out.

A weekend such as this is an excellent time to give your groomsmen their thank-you gifts. A new spinning reel, a fillet knife, or a new tacklebox are appropriate to the occasion and will be appreciated by your fishing buddies.

Casino Night _____

Las Vegas or Monte Carlo are as close as your living room or basement recreation room. One groom's attendants organized a casino night. Tickets sold to this exclusive event paid for the gaming tables and refreshments, which included beer, hot dogs, soft drinks, and assorted snacks.

Several different tables were set up, and a dealer was assigned to each table. Participants played seven-card stud, five-card draw, twenty-one, and blackjack. Winners were allowed to keep their winnings; however, when the dealer won, the proceeds went to the groom.

If gambling is illegal in your state, or if you're uncomfortable playing for money, use poker chips instead of money. At the end of the evening, players can use their chips to "buy" prizes such as pocket knives and tape measures. Door prizes such as mini-coolers can also be awarded throughout the evening.

Take Me Out to the Ballgame ___

An evening at a professional sporting event is just the ticket for a prewedding get-together for the groom and his attendants.

Round up the guys and head for the local ballpark or stadium. For extra-special viewing, rent box seats. Although you may want to stop for dinner before the game, why not eat at the ballpark? Hot dogs or bratwurst smothered in ketchup and relish or mustard and sauerkraut always taste better at the stadium. Don't forget the popcorn, or nachos dripping with cheese.

Stop off at your favorite pub after the game to discuss the evening's big plays.

Groom's Bicycle Marathon _____

Get the groomsmen and ushers into shape for the wedding day by joining a bicycle marathon. (To make it more meaningful, do it for a charitable organization.) Or, stage a marathon of your own. Practice together before the race.

After the ride, stop at a take-out restaurant and buy a bucket of fried chicken, biscuits, and cole slaw and have a picnic at a nearby park.

Commemorate the event by giving your attendants and ushers a thank-you gift — perhaps tire pumps or racing gloves. Or give each of them a specially made T-shirt with your name and the bride's printed on it below the words, "Prenuptial Bicycle Marathon."

Health Club Workout _____

Take the guys to your health-and-fitness club for some pre-wedding exercise.

Jog around the track or work out on the weight machine. Bask in the sauna and whirlpool and cool off in the swimming pool before getting a relaxing massage. It's a great way to calm wedding nerves.

At the end of the session, give each of your attendants a good-quality sports bag as a thank-you gift.

Tuxes Tonight _____

If tuxedos are to be rented for the ceremony, getting fitted is one of the major duties of the groom and his men. Make it an occasion for a celebration as well.

Pick a time that's convenient for all the groomsmen. If your dad and hers are wearing tuxes, be sure to include them. You can make the ringbearer feel grown-up and important, too, by bringing him along.

Make dinner reservations at a local steakhouse. Meet at the formal-wear shop to have your measurements taken. Then cruise over to the steakhouse for dinner, drinks, and lots of guy talk. If you like, order a special cake for dessert to commemorate the occasion.

This is a good time to present your groomsmen with their thank-you gifts, and it's a good way to make certain everyone is ready for the big day.

Audition Tour

Here's one way to have fun with the guys and perform a practical service as well.

Hire a van with a nondrinking chauffeur to take you and your groomsmen on a tour of local bars and nightclubs. The chauffeur will relieve you of driving and parking worries. The purpose: To audition bands or musicians for the wedding reception.

If your community publishes an entertainment guide, you can use it to direct you to various nightclubs around town. The guide may also help you find agencies that provide musicians for parties and weddings. Some agencies now provide videotapes so you can audition several groups at once. Sit back, relax and watch the show. At the end of the evening, ask your attendants to vote for the group they like best.

If the bride's family is paying for the reception entertainment, be sure to ask how much they have budgeted for music, and keep that figure in mind when auditioning groups.

Groom's Racquetball Tournament

If you play handball or racquetball, invite your attendants to join you on the court for a lively game or two. Reserve the courts ahead of time so the games can be played simultaneously. Keep the competition friendly — after all, these guys will be standing behind you at the altar.

After the workout, head for the showers and then out to a favorite restaurant. Over drinks, give your groomsmen their thank-you gifts — a certificate for a trial membership at the club, perhaps.

Boys' Toys Shower

A new household needs many items, and tools are a very necessary part of keeping any home running smoothly.

The best man should host this all-male shower. Unless you enjoy cooking, a simple menu works best. A visit to your supermarket deli department will yield a selection of cold cuts and cheeses, salads, and crisp dill pickles. Set out a variety of breads and sandwich spreads and you've got a bachelor's buffet. Have plenty of cold beer on hand.

To make invitations, cut pictures of tools out of a tool catalog and glue them to a prestamped postcard (available at your local post office). Under the picture, write, "Help Fill Jim's Toolbox." Give the date, place, and time of the party. Write the guest's address on the other side. Be sure to invite the father of the bride as well as the groom's father. If the wedding party includes a ringbearer, make him feel special by asking him to attend, too.

Although some power tools, such as radial arm saws, can be very expensive, the tools the groom will need most often are smaller hand tools — hammers, cordless drills and screw-drivers, plumber's wrenches, electronic stud finders. Also good are tool belts, socket sets, pocket-size levels, an assortment of nails and screws, and an organizer with small plastic drawers to hold nuts and bolts. If the groom enjoys woodworking, you can give him more specialized tools such as chisels, clamps, and sanders.

Give whatever you wish. But be sure to buy high-quality tools that will give dependable service.

9. Rehearsal Dinners

*T*he groom or his family traditionally gives the rehearsal dinner, but that doesn't mean it has to follow a prescribed program or take place in a traditional setting.

Pirate's Beach Party

Head to the beach for this memorable rehearsal dinner.

Provide directions to the beach by drawing a map on parchment paper (burn the edges with a match to give it an authentic look).

Stab a pole into the sand and hoist the Jolly Roger. Spread checkered tablecloths out on the beach. While the grills are heating, serve shrimp cocktail from coolers disguised as treasure chests. Drinks containing rum, such as Bacardi cocktails or rum and colas with a twist of lime, are appropriate before-dinner refreshments. Fry fresh fish for the main course, or grill salmon steaks. Dessert should be — what else? — rum cake!

Bring along a cassette deck and play some Reggae music or old Harry Belafonte tunes such as "Jamaica."

Children who are to be wedding attendants will be thrilled to attend the rehearsal dinner. To keep little ones (and their parents) busy while the food is being prepared, arm them with plastic shovels and send them on a treasure hunt. Bury little boxes of toy jewelry or gold, foil-wrapped chocolate coins. Give the kids an easy-to-follow treasure map and turn them loose.

Great Gatsby Photographer's Studio

A rehearsal dinner in a good, but otherwise ordinary, restaurant will take on a special quality when you hire a photographer who specializes in "old-time" portraiture.

Have one end of a large banquet room set up as the photographer's studio where members of the wedding party can have their photos taken in period costumes. (You'll need to provide a place for them to change clothes.) Arrange to have the photographer arrive at the banquet site an hour ahead of time. This will give him or her time to set up lights and props and get the costumes ready for guests to try on. Although there is a limit to the amount of gear one person can bring to a party, the photographer should have a full range of costumes, custom scenes, cutout boards, and other props to give the photos an antique look.

Imagine the maid of honor costumed as a dance hall girl, or your son dressed as Wyatt Earp. Watching each other pose for the camera is sure to provide some laughs as guests nibble on hors d'ouevres before dinner. Give each person (or couple) a copy of the photo as a souvenir of the evening.

If you can't find an old-time photographer in your area, ask your guests to come dressed in Roaring Twenties costume. Then look for a photography studio that advertises fast film processing. You can have photos taken early in the evening and get them back before your guests go home.

Heritage Rehearsal Dinner ———

Whether you're French, English, Japanese, Swedish, Hawaiian, Native American, or Russian, let your heritage (and your menu) set the stage for a wonderful at-home evening celebrating your roots. This theme can be adapted to fit any ethnic group.

Persons of German ancestry can celebrate the *Polterabend* — an "evening of uproar" — the night before the wedding. It features firecrackers, banging pans, and breaking crockery. Since showers are not a German custom, guests frequently bring their gifts (or have them delivered) on the *Polterabend*.

Because Germans typically eat a large dinner at noon and a cold supper, you may want to serve *Mittagessen* at night. Start with chicken soup, followed by fried *spätzle* noodles and roast pork or veal surrounded by potatoes and one or two other vegetables. Serve a fine Rhine wine. For a truly authentic dessert, serve bread pudding or a compote of stewed fruits. Toast the bridal couple with more Rhine wine or with steins of imported German beer. (Steins also make terrific flower vases.)

If you're Irish, set the table with an emerald green tablecloth and napkins. White stoneware makes a simple but striking contrast. Tie a shiny green ribbon around small pots of shamrocks and put them at each place at the table. Guests can take them home as favors.

Dinner is hearty Irish fare: corned beef with cabbage, turnips, onions, potatoes, carrots, and parsnips served with Irish soda bread and mustard sauce on the side. Follow with jam cake for dessert and Irish coffee topped with a dollop of whipped cream. Or get extravagant and serve Madigan's Velvet Trousers, a pudding made of gelatin, whipping cream, honey, and Irish whiskey.

After dinner, gather around the piano and sing sentimental tunes such as "Danny Boy," "When Irish Eyes Are Smilin'," and "The Black Velvet Band."

Scandinavian celebrants will enjoy a *smorgasbord* of baked ham, brown beans, rice pudding, pickled herring, *sylta*, Swedish meatballs, several cheeses, and *potatis korv* — sausage made of ground pork and potatoes. Top it off with *krumkake* and hot, steaming coffee.

Decorate the center of the table with a red Dala horse or runners made of hardanger embroidery. Display native costumes on a wall or on a dressmaker's form.

By taking bits and pieces of your ethnic heritage, you can put together a wonderful party theme and create a memorable evening for your son, his wife-to-be, and his future in-laws. As you can see, the possibilities are endless!

Rollin' on the River

Cruising around a body of water and watching the sun go down is a fine way to relieve some of those prenuptial jitters — for you and all the members of the wedding party.

If your community is surrounded by lakes or has a river running through it, boats may be available for charter. Some boats may accommodate more than 100, others fewer than 25. Some can provide a catered meal and a live band, while others provide a floating party room to which you can bring your own food, beverages, and taped music.

To provide a real "Mark Twain" atmosphere, hire a banjo player to entertain your dinner guests with Dixieland flair. If this is a catered affair, ask the charter company if it can provide decorations as well as champagne for the toast. If you are the caterer, try to board the boat early to put up some appropriate decorations. You may also want to sneak down shore and place some "Good Wishes" signs where you can beam the boat's spotlight at them as you sail past.

Invitations can be issued on copies of your state's water-safety rules. (Contact your state department of natural resources for a sample.) Or wrap the invitation around a roll of Life Savers™ candy.

Whether you host the rehearsal dinner or your parents take care of the bill, make sure that food and drink are plentiful. Everyone appreciates a generous bridegroom. (If you're piloting the boat, remember not to imbibe too much. Some states have passed "drunken boater" laws that carry stiff fines.)

After the toasts, sit back and watch the stars come out. What a pleasant way to spend your postrehearsal hours!

Wild Game Rehearsal Dinner ___

Does your son live for the opening of hunting season? Does he spend hours training his dog to point or retrieve? Is he more at home in the woods than in the big city? Use a Wild Game Rehearsal Dinner to please the palate and show off the hunting prowess of your Great White Hunter.

Decorate your dining room with wildlife art and duck decoys, or cut photos of deer, antelope, and fish from wildlife magazines. Use a red tablecloth and napkins, and place a bright red-and-green plaid runner down the center of the table. For a centerpiece, put local flora such as cattails, strawflowers or chrysanthemums inside the bell of a hunting horn. (If you can't find a hunting horn, you may be able to round up an old French horn at a music or antique store.)

Complete the table decorations by placing small duck or goose Christmas ornaments next to each water glass. Guests can take these home as favors.

For appetizers, start with sausage made from deer or antelope (best if the groom has killed the game himself) and a variety of hearty cheeses. For the main course, serve smoked pheasant, wild duck roasted in orange juice and thinly slice onions, or venison smothered in a hearty sauce of burgundy and mushrooms. Have a wild rice pilaf and green beans amandine on the side.

To complete the hunting-lodge atmosphere, set a crackling fire in the fireplace and have the bridal couple read aloud some hunting scenes from Ernest Hemingway's Snows of Kilimanjaro.

After the reading, the father of the groom should toast the couple. He may say something like, "Son, we've hunted together for many years now. It's been fun watching you grow up, to learn how to handle firearms safely, and become a responsible hunter. However, this latest hunting trip was something you had to do on your own, and I must say you were very successful. I'm very happy to welcome Mary into our family. My best to the both of you."

This special salute to his hunting skills is an evening your son will remember for many autumn nights to come.

Aviator's Rehearsal Dinner ____

A groom with a private pilot's license is probably happiest when he's at the airport flying or making hangar talk. A rehearsal dinner in an airplane hangar is bound to be a memorable affair.

If you don't own your own plane and hangar, make arrangements to rent hangar space at a local airport where you rent your planes. The rental cost will depend on the size of the hangar, and you may be required to sign an insurance waiver to use the building. For safety's sake, keep young guests such as the flower girl and ringbearer away from the planes. With the owner's permission, set up tables between the airplanes. Drape the tables with brightly colored paper tablecloths, and use small model airplanes or inexpensive balsa gliders as place card holders. Bring in your own food, or have it catered.

If the groom plans to give your guests after-dinner flights around the airport, remember the FAA restrictions on the consumption of alcoholic beverages, and use sparkling catawba juice instead of champagne for the toasts.

The best man could offer the first toast, saying, "Ralph worked long and hard to get his pilot's license. I'll never forget how excited he was when he called me to tell me about his first solo flight. It's nice to know that after tomorrow, he won't be flying solo any more."

After more toasts and congratulatory remarks, the groom and his bride-to-be can guide their guests to a waiting airplane for a series of short, starry-night flights. It's an evening everyone will remember.

"Camelot"

One father planned a very special rehearsal dinner. He reserved a room at a restaurant with English Tudor decor, then rolled out the red carpet for the groom and his queen-to-be. The couple and their attendants were treated royally throughout the dinner. Afterward, the court was entertained by a juggler and a strolling minstrel.

You can create a similar evening for your son and his bride-to-be. Make reservations at a local restaurant noted for its prime rib or baron of beef. If the decor already has an English look to it, you're ahead of the game. If not, create your own English court.

Seat guests at round tables *a la* King Arthur. Members of the wedding party should be seated at a long table at one end of the room. To make the guests of honor more visible, have the table placed on risers.

Garlands of flowers are an important part of the decor for this theme. String long ropes of them from the ceiling and make crowns of flowers for the women in the wedding party to wear in their hair.

To give the evening a truly Elizabethan flavor, have members of the wedding party read passages from Shakespeare — the balcony scene from "Romeo and Juliet," perhaps, or Oberon's final speech in "A Midsummer Night's Dream." You can find magicians and jugglers in the Yellow Pages, and you may be lucky enough to find musicians who specialize in Renaissance or medieval music through your local college or music school, or through a talent agency.

For the toast, present the couple with a French *coupe de mariage*, a two-handled cup they can pass down to their children.

With all this activity, this rehearsal dinner will shine brightly in the memories of both families for years to come.

Skating Fantasy

One groom-to-be had played hockey nearly all his life — from the bantam league through high school. It was fitting, then, for his rehearsal dinner to take place on the ice.

A school bus collected all the guests and took them to a local ice arena. A temporary floor had been built over the ice rink, and tables and chairs were set up on the platform. Dinner was catered. Ice skates, hockey sticks, and jerseys were all part of the decor for this memorable evening.

To host your own "Skating Fantasy," rent a local ice or roller-skating rink. Send "tickets" to your guests to invite them to the event. If the dinner will be held at an ice arena, remind guests to wear warm clothing and shoes. Dress should be casual — appropriate for a hockey game. For fun, supply guests with hockey jerseys or T-shirts imprinted with the names of the groom's favorite team. Put little pennants with the bride's and groom's names on them on the table as favors.

Have guests meet at your home for cocktails and appetizers. At the appropriate time, have a school bus or van pull up to your front door to transport everyone to the ice arena. Check with your charter company; it may be more economical to have the bus wait for your group rather than leave and come back when the evening's festivities are finished.

If the bride and groom are both accomplished skaters, they can add some romance to the evening by performing an impromptu dance across the ice.

Aprés-Rehearsal Ski Dinner

If the groom has schussed the powder at Vail, reflect his skiing interest by holding the rehearsal dinner at a ski lodge.

Invite guests with a "lift ticket" you make yourself. Cut tags from lightweight cardboard. Punch a hole in the top of each tag, run some yarn through the hole, and tie the ends together. On the tag, write the date, time, and location of the party. Be sure to include instructions on dress. If necessary, draw a map on the back of the ticket and give guests instructions on how to get to the party.

To set the tone for the evening, give guests a ride on the ski lift. Then move the party to the lodge for dinner. If the dinner takes place in winter, guests will appreciate a warm-up of Tom and Jerrys or hot, buttered rum. In summer, a gathering on the deck will keep everyone cool.

Favors at the dinner table can include small skier Christmas tree ornaments (you can find them at gift shops that sell Christmas items year-round). Decorate the room with paper snowflakes you cut out yourself.

After dinner, gather before the chalet fireplace for toasts to the bride and groom.

VCR Viewing Night

Here's an idea for a small wedding party.

Hold an intimate buffet dinner for the wedding party in your home. After dinner, turn on the VCR and show guests old home movies and slides (transferred to videotape) of the bride and groom's childhoods. After the trip down memory lane, if everyone is still game, show a romantic movie such as "Casablanca" or "An Officer and a Gentleman."

Pop a big batch of popcorn and enjoy the show.

Pizza Party

If casual is your style, and your wedding party's not overly large, then a pizza party may be your perfect rehearsal dinner.

Assemble all the ingredients — sausage, pepperoni, green peppers, black olives, onion slices, cheeses, and sauce — and set them out in bowls on a table. Make your own crusts or use commercially prepared crusts (sometimes available from bakeries or in butcher shops.) (English muffins make excellent crusts for individual pizzas.) Then let guests prepare their own pizzas. Toss a salad and have plenty of Chianti on hand. For dessert, serve a different kind of "pizza" — a large, chocolate chip cookie covered with marshmallow "cheese."

For a musical backdrop, go to the library and check out music by Italian composers — Verdi, Vivaldi, Rossini. If their music is too classical for your taste, look for folk dance music that includes lively tarantellas. Or get schmaltzy with "Arrividerci Roma." Whatever your choice, you'll be feeling very Italian by the end of the evening.

Wedding Roast

In between courses at a good local restaurant, stage a roast of the bridal couple. The best man acts as emcee.

Now's the time to drag out the old home movies, the pictures of the groom lying on a bearskin rug, the school photos. All those things you swore you'd never let the bride live down. Time for Dad to use some of his best barbs.

You may want to do some role playing, with Mom and little sister acting out the parts of parent and child. Keep it light and friendly, and let the couple know you still love them in spite of their faults.

At the end of the evening, offer up a more traditional wedding toast, wishing the bride and groom all the best in their new lives together.

"Family Feud"

If your two tribes can take some good-natured ribbing and can give as good as they get, then use the rehearsal dinner to play a bridal version of the popular television game "Family Feud."

Before dinner, assemble a list of questions about each family. During the cocktail hour, form two lines on opposite sides of the banquet room, either by family or "boys against girls." Have the best man or maid of honor act as moderator, and let the games begin!

You could also form family teams to play Pictionary™, with members taking turns defining the words on a large pad of paper set upon an easel.

End the games with a toast to the bride and groom as a signal to begin the dinner.

Candlelight Barbecue Rehearsal Dinner _____

One groom's mother found a way to enjoy a summer evening by holding the rehearsal dinner out-of-doors. To make it even more special, she placed candles all over the backyard. Guests enjoyed a delicious barbecue in an intimate candlelight setting — a perfect way to relax before the wedding.

You can stage a similar event in your own backyard. If you live in an area where mosquitoes and gnats prevail at dusk, spray the party area with a bug bomb about one hour before guests arrive. Outline the patio or lawn with torches. For further insect control, place citronella candles on low tables throughout the yard.

Decorate the area with Chinese paper lanterns, or string tiny Christmas lights through the trees and bushes. Hang wind chimes to catch the night breeze.

Set up a buffet table at one end of the yard. Have guests pick up trays at the beginning of the line. On each tray, place a tiny vigil light in a decorative holder painted with the names of the bride and groom. Let guests take the candles home as party favors.

If you seat your guests at tables, place a plumber's candle (available at hardware stores) in a hurricane lamp in the center of each table. Plumber's candles are inexpensive and burn a long time, and the lamp globe will protect the flame from any sudden gusts of wind.

Let the party wind down naturally as people head for home and rest before the next day's ceremony.

Road Rally Rehearsal Dinner __

This scavenger hunt on wheels could take some time, so if you're worried about getting plenty of sleep before the wedding, hold your rehearsal two days before the wedding, or schedule your church rehearsal early in the day.

At the conclusion of the rehearsal, separate all the members of the wedding party and supporting cast (spouses, parents, etc.) into teams and have them get into cars. Provide each team with a set of instructions such as "Drive to the convenience store on Melrose and Lake Street and buy a pack of chewing gum. The cashier will give you instructions for the next leg of the journey." At each stop, players get a clue to the next destination. You may want to include a stop at a bar for a predinner drink (the bartender gives out the clue that leads to the final destination). The idea is to have everyone end up at the restaurant where the rehearsal dinner will take place. The first team to complete all the clues and reach the restaurant wins.

Provide a *good* prize for the winners to encourage everyone to get to the dinner on time. Have gag gifts ready for the laggards and for those who have the funniest experience while on the road.

Down-Home Rehearsal Dinner _____

Bring your rehearsal dinner to the country.

Issue the invitation on ears of dried corn (a florist should be able to get them for you). Write the party information — date, time, and place — on the corn with a felt-tip marking pen. After the ink has dried, place the ears into cardboard tubes for mailing. Have folks dress casually in jeans and plaid sports shirts. As a party favor, supply everyone with a cap from a seed corn company.

Decorate the party room with bales of hay, grain scoops, and pitchforks (available at rural feed stores). Wooden picnic tables can be covered with checkered cloths, and food can be served from wicker picnic baskets.

Build or rent a large barbecue pit and roast a whole pig. For dessert, offer your guests their choice of apple, berry, or lemon meringue pie. (If you're not an accomplished baker, make it easy on yourself and purchase the pies at a local bakery.)

After dinner, hold an old-fashioned barn dance to the accompaniment of a fiddle, guitar, or accordion. Hire a caller to lead you through the Virginia reel, two-step, or square dance.

Before the evening ends, get a group together and serenade the bridal couple with a jug or kazoo band. Provide rhythm accompaniment for the musicians with an old washboard or spoons.

Fishing Frolic

Maybe you've scheduled your wedding close to the start of fishing season. Or maybe the season's a long way off. If there's a trout farm or pool near you, hold your rehearsal dinner there. Many of these farms have a restaurant nearby, where guests can catch their own meal. Wetting a line is in season all year long!

Those families who want to include children at the rehearsal dinner will enjoy the activity. This is a fun theme for the junior set, as well as the adults.

Invite guests by giving them a "license" to fish at the farm. It could read something like this:

Department of Natural Resources
Angling License

In consideration of the fact that _____ (guest's name) is a member of the wedding party of_____ and _____ (bride and groom), applicant is licensed to take fish by angling during the evening of _____ (date) at Trout Farm, 7:00 p.m. to 10:00 p.m.

County of _____

State of _____

Fill a fisherman's creel with fresh flowers for the centerpiece at the head table. Tie tiny flies or other small fishing lures to place cards (for youngsters, you may want to remove the hooks). For favors, paint the names of the bride and groom on bright plastic bobbers. To give your party a truly aquatic feel, cut fish shapes from construction paper and suspend them from the party room ceiling with transparent fishing line.

The entertainment for the evening is already provided as guests drop a line into the trout stream. Children will be especially thrilled to catch their own dinner, which is cooked on the premises. And, because the restaurant has a supply of fresh-caught fish on hand, even the luckless fisherman will be able to enjoy the catch of the day. This is one fishing trip where everybody catches the big one.

Evening Musicale _____

If the bride and groom are musicians, they'll appreciate a rehearsal dinner highlighted by a prewedding concert. This elegant affair can be held in a fine restaurant or in a garden setting.

Start with cocktails and hors d'ouevres accompanied by a string trio or woodwind quartet playing classical compositions. Or hire a group of strolling musicians to play show tunes and other popular music for guests upon request. Since most such groups are booked for two-hour performances, you'll have music throughout the cocktail and dinner hours.

When decorating, go for a sophisticated black-and-white look. Use cocktail napkins printed with a piano key design (usually available at paper-supply stores). Cover tables with white cloths, and, for dramatic effect, use black napkins. Use brass note holders in the shape of a treble clef both as place card holders and as a party favor. Look for them in stationery shops or in stores that sell musical instruments. Many now carry gift items for musicians.

Create a bower for the couple to sit in after dinner. Buy 1-foot-wide lattices at a building supply store or lumberyard and nail them together to form an arch. Spray-paint the lattices white. Build a musical staff out of thin pieces of wood (five lines down and two on each side), spray them black, and attach them to the lattices. Entwine each staff with flower "notes." Place a bench (a piano bench will do) under the arch for seating.

After dinner, gather the couple's musical friends, and stage an operetta that tells the story of their courtship. Or have a duet or quartet serenade them with a variety of love songs. Be sure to include their "special" song.

10. Miscellaneous Parties

Weddings require a lot of preparation. With proper planning, everything can go off without a hitch. Getting ready should be fun. So should readying your new home. Plan to enjoy every step of the way!

Wedding Planning Party ─────────

You've announced your engagement to your family and all your friends. The date is set and the church or synagogue is reserved. Between today and the wedding day, you have a lot of work to do. If they haven't already met, now's the time for the parents of the bride to bring the two sets of parents together.

You'll have much to discuss. Do it over big platters of spaghetti and meatballs or fettucini alfredo, an antipasto salad, and crusty garlic bread. Complement the meal with a robust Chianti. For dessert, serve spumoni, anise cookies, and espresso.

Use your everyday dishes, but put a cheery cloth on the table and place a big bouquet of fresh flowers in the center, flanked by tall white candles.

During dinner, run down the list of particulars. What time will the ceremony take place? How many attendants will there be? What music will be played? How many guests will attend from each side of the family? What color will the bridesmaids' dresses be? What color (or colors) will the mothers wear? Will the fathers wear tuxedos? Where will the reception be held? Who will pay for the use of the hall — the bridal couple, or the bride's parents? Who will pay for the refreshments at the reception? When will the rehearsal be?

Inviting Made Easy

Wedding invitations should be addressed by hand. But, writing out 300 or more invitations all by yourself is a big job (and a major cause of writer's cramp!)

Invite your friends to an invitation work party. Serve nongreasy snacks and soft drinks. Be sure to have plenty of stamps and a damp sponge handy for sealing envelopes.

Form an assembly line. Have the calligraphers or those with the best handwriting address the envelopes in dark blue or black ink. Have the others do the stuffing, sealing, and stamping. Make sure someone checks the finished invitations against the list to be sure you don't leave anyone out.

Royal Taster's Party

Gather a panel of select friends to taste-test two or three wedding cakes and icings, as well as two or three varieties of chilled champagne.

Keep in mind that many couples today want something other than a traditional white wedding cake. Under that fancy frosting may lurk a dark chocolate confection. Some couples are using a raspberry mousse filling between the layers. The cake may reflect the theme of the wedding ceremony. Or it may give a nod to the couple's ethnic heritage, such as an Austrian *sacher torte* or Scandinavian *kronsekage*. Serve small portions of the different cakes so that tasters can make a good judgment without getting too full. Color-code each champagne sample and ask your guests to vote for their favorites.

If you're having a hard time deciding on the hors d'ouevres menu, you may also wish to purchase a "preview platter" from the caterer for your guests to sample.

Pass the plastic forks, plates, and napkins and enjoy! (But be ready to draw straws in case of a tie!)

Favor Assembly Party

Gather your friends and form an assembly line to put together favors for the wedding reception. (*Somebody's* got to fill all those little net bags with bird seed!)

Have one person cut up the groom's cake while another boxes it. Have another wrap sugar-coated almonds (symbolizing the bitter and sweet parts of married life) in tiny gift boxes that guests can take home with them. Those with artistic flair can work on making centerpieces for each table. If your guest list is not large, you may want to make silk boutonnieres for each of your wedding guests.

Treat workers to dessert and coffee after the work is through.

For more ideas on favors, consult Wedding Plans: 50 Unique Themes for the Wedding of Your Dreams by Sharon Dlugosch, Brighton Publications, Inc., P.O. Box 12706, New Brighton, MN 55112.

Wedding Party Mixer ───────

One couple solved the problem of introducing members of the wedding party to each other by holding a party for the wedding party.

Both sets of parents, parents of the wedding party members (most were family friends) as well as the attendants were invited to an afternoon on the beach. Invitees could also bring guests if they chose. Water-skiing, volleyball, and suntanning were among the activities offered. Barbecued chicken and steaks were the main menu items.

Sharing Memories Party ───────

In the hustle and bustle of preparing for a wedding, it's sometimes easy to forget that your best man may not know the maid of honor, or that the groom's parents may not have met the parents of the flower girl. Give them all a chance to meet and mingle at an informal get-together *before* the big rehearsal.

Choose an evening when most members of your wedding party are free. Set out a light spread of hors d'ouevres and cocktails, or serve a backyard barbecue. Or, invite everyone over for dessert and coffee. It doesn't have to be fancy, just fun!

Ask each person to bring the oldest pictures they have of the bride and groom. For parents, of course, this means baby pictures. For school chums, it could mean the first day at college; for co-workers, an on-the-job scene. As the pictures are passed around, each person explains his or her relationship to the couple.

There is sure to be lots of laughter as guests swap stories and trade jokes (let's hope they're not *all* at your expense!). Your friends will make new friends, and there won't be any strangers in your wedding party!

Mixed-Doubles Golf Tournament

If you and your groom are from different cities or states, and your attendants don't know each other, plan a sporting event. Head out to your nearest par-three or miniature golf course for an afternoon of fun.

This is one tournament where being good doesn't count. Award a prize to the person who lands a ball *farthest* from the pin on hole 5. Offer a crying towel to the one whose ball doesn't quite make it over the water hazard, and a child's toy rake and shovel to the player who gets stuck in the sand trap. Give a wristwatch-style scorekeeper to the one who racks up the highest score. As party favors, give everyone a set of golf tees or golf balls imprinted with the names of the bride and groom.

Keep some cold drinks in the cart to quench everyone's thirst. When everyone has finished the front nine, head back to the clubhouse for sandwiches, drinks, and lots of talk.

Shall We Dance?

What is more memorable or more romantic than the newly-weds' first twirl around the dance floor?

If your waltz step could use a bit of brushing up, take your bridal party to a prewedding dance lesson. Make an appointment at a local dance studio, or take your group to a local ballroom to give everyone some dance pointers.

Pair up dancers as you would in the bridal procession, with the maid of honor dancing with the best man, and so on. Then have everyone change partners. You may even want to include the flower girl and ringbearer.

After the lesson, dance to more familiar music, and serve some light refreshments.

Don't be too concerned about form. Just get out there and enjoy dancing to the beat.

Gardener's Party _____

If you're planning an outdoor wedding, you'd like your yard to look its best. You don't need to hire a private gardener. A few helping hands is all it takes to go from jungle to Garden of Eden.

Provide equipment for your workers — lawn mowers, pruning shears, edge trimmers and trash bags — as well as plenty of cool drinks throughout the day.

Give each person a choice of tasks to complete throughout the day — weeding the flower beds, raking the lawn, setting up an arbor for the ceremony. Edge the lawns so they look neat and tidy. Pinch the dead blossoms off the marigolds. Put black plastic under the shrubs and fill the in-between spaces with wood chips or crushed rock. Fill in any other bare spots with potted plants. If you're really ambitious, plant a tree to commemorate the wedding!

When all the work is done, "order in" Chinese take-out food and let everyone enjoy a feast of chicken wings, fried rice, and egg rolls.

When your guests arrive for the wedding, they'll be in a true garden paradise!

Deck the Hall _____

Here's another opportunity to turn work into an occasion. On the morning of the wedding, whisk a decorating crew to the reception site. Bring along your camera for some candid shots of your friends and relatives as they hang streamers, inflate balloons, arrange table skirts, and place other decorations around the hall. Imagine the contrast in your wedding photo album — your maid of honor in hair rollers, jeans, and a T-shirt in the morning and formal hat and gown in the evening!

Now is a good time for a last-minute consultation with the custodian to make sure you have enough tables and chairs for all your guests and to make sure the florist delivers your flowers on time.

Coffee, juice, and breakfast rolls or muffins should give your workers plenty of energy to get the job done.

Wedding Photo Party _____

To save time and confusion and to have the bridal party looking its photographic best, many brides hold their photo sessions *before* the ceremony. If it's a large wedding party and you're shooting both sides of the family, the photo session may run as long as two hours.

As a thoughtful gesture, provide some light refreshments for the people who are waiting their turn under the photographer's lights. The refreshments not only reduce tension, but help pass the time before the ceremony.

Serve sparkling water, raw vegetables, sliced apples, and crackers and cheese. Avoid messy dips and spreads and dark-colored beverages such as grape juice or fruit punch that could stain your flower girl's frilly pink dress.

A Moving Celebration _____

Moving to a new home is exciting. It is also a lot of work. But work can seem like play if you organize a party.

Pack everything in advance. Label all the boxes so movers can take them directly to the rooms where they will be unpacked. Make sure you have phone service in both your old and new homes on the day of the move, just in case you need to reach one another. Be sure to rent a truck or van large enough to carry all your possessions in one trip. (This will save you both time and money.) Organize your helpers so some are putting boxes and furniture on the rental truck at the old house. Have others stationed in your new home, ready to unpack as soon as the truck arrives. (If you can, get them to help clean the new house before the loaded truck arrives.)

Be ready with refreshments and a selection of fast, rhythmic music to make the job go faster and seem easier.

Working Party

The pioneers had the right idea when they built a log cabin or put up a barn; they did it *together.* You may not be building a barn, but wouldn't it be nice to have some help painting the window trim or wallpapering the kitchen?

After the wedding, invite your handy friends over by sending the invitation wrapped around a thin artist's paintbrush. Tell them how they can exchange it for a larger brush — and a meal — by helping you redecorate.

Let the jacks-of-all-trades handle jobs such as changing locks or installing a new garbage disposal. Have the experienced wallpaper hanger show others how to do the corners. Hand a paintbrush or roller to the neatnik. The one with the artistic hand can hang the drapes.

Keep the soft drinks coming. When the work is finished, offer your friends sloppy Joes or slices of barbecued ham on buns, corn chips, a tossed salad, and beverages in return for their labor.

Housewarming

A housewarming is another party you host, but this one requires no effort on the part of your guests. It's really an opportunity to show off your new home.

Send out invitations shaped like little houses with a door that opens. Inside, specify the date and time and write a message that says something like, "Come see our new home!" which implies that gifts are not required. Be prepared to give several tours of the premises. Serve light refreshments such as punch and cookies.

Housewarming parties can also be surprise parties for the new couple (but keep your fingers crossed and hope the house is clean!). Have friends take the couple out on a shopping spree (or invent some other ruse). While the foursome is gone, have everyone else gather at the new house. When the friends return, the party's on!

A potluck dinner or picnic works best for this type of surprise party.

Gifts are optional, but practical articles such as doormats, house plants or an engraved brass door knocker are appropriate.

New Neighbors Welcome Party

A couple who've spent the day hoisting furniture off the moving van isn't going to be too interested in cooking dinner. So gather the neighbors and take dinner to them. It's a great way to get acquainted.

Neighbors may also want to bring a small, useful gift for setting up housekeeping, such as a package of light bulbs, an assortment of screws and nails, a flashlight, or a new garbage can.

Also handy would be an address book with the names and addresses of the neighbors and neighborhood businesses such as a bakery or deli, veterinarian, plumber, or drugstore.

To give the couple an all-out welcome, hold a square dance in the driveway. Hire a caller to lead everyone through the dances or play a private collection of square dance records or tapes.

11. Wedding Weekend

*M*ore and more families are joining the trend toward savoring the days around the wedding, stretching the celebration out beyond the day of the ceremony to become a celebration of the family. Although most weddings take place on Saturday, it's not uncommon for a family to come together on Friday night, spend Saturday together, and attend the wedding on Sunday.

Regional Buffet Bash _____

Meet your guests at the airport, train, or bus station and present them with an itinerary for the weekend. Though it might include a Saturday morning brunch, or a football game (and of course, the wedding), begin with a casual Friday night buffet.

Once you have collected your guests, transported them to their accommodations, and made them generally comfortable, treat them to a pleasant evening. Games and good food are proven icebreakers.

Begin the evening by having your guests play a game of bingo. Guests are handed a bingo card with a set of clues printed in each square. They must then talk to each person in the crowd and get their signatures as they match people to clues. For example, "He's a dentist in California." The first person to complete a row wins a prize.

Next give your visitors something to talk about by introducing them to the area's cuisine.

For example, blackened fish, dirty rice, seafood creole, and Louisiana bread pudding are examples of Cajun cooking.

In New England, Boston baked beans, chicken pie, turkey with oyster stuffing, cod cakes, Indian rye bread, and Colonial wafers capped with whipped cream and applesauce are menu features.

Looking south, of course, there is Southern fried chicken, corn bread, black-eyed peas, biscuits and red-eye gravy, and maybe a Georgia peach pie.

In the Midwest, serve broiled walleye, wild rice pilaf, and blueberry muffins; or prime rib of beef and corn on the cob.

Those who live in the desert Southwest may want to serve pork stew with cornbread stuffing, sea bass baked in foil and flavored with cilantro, or green chili stew with lamb and juniper berries.

Whatever your region's culinary claim to fame, you're sure to provide a taste sensation that guests will remember for quite some time!

Friday Night Fiesta _____

Mexican food has become such a mainstay in the American diet that it is easy to overlook our south-of-the-border neighbors when looking for a party theme.

Drape the party room with travel posters depicting the Aztec pyramids, Cancun, and the Mexican flag. String green, red, and white streamers — the colors of the Mexican flag — so they radiate from the center of the ceiling to the outer edges of the room. Hang a candy-and-gift-filled piñata from the center.

Provide the proper musical backdrop by hiring a mariachi band. If that's too expensive, check out some mariachi records from the library, or play some old Herb Alpert and the Tijuana Brass LPs.

For appetizers, serve nachos with guacamole and cheese and big, frosty margaritas. (Have a lemon-lime drink available for the kids.)

Keep the atmosphere informal by setting up a tostada bar where guests can help themselves to the fixings for tortillas, enchiladas and refried beans. For dessert, serve sopaipillas and ice cream and coffee spiked with brandy, Kahlua, and chocolate syrup, topped with cinnamon-flavored whipped cream.

After dinner, blindfold the kids, give them a broom handle, and let them swing away at the piñata. Be ready for a mad scramble when the piñata breaks and its contents scatter across the floor.

Wedding-Morning Breakfast

Out-of-town guests will especially appreciate this wake-up call.

Invite them to breakfast with a handwritten note tucked in with the wedding invitation. If you've already had several bridal showers, perhaps an aunt could host this event for you. (Since the groom, by tradition, is not supposed to see the bride before the wedding, perhaps his family could hold a similar, separate breakfast for travelers from his side of the family.)

Set the table with everyday stoneware. Or give your table an eclectic look by mixing different patterns of china. Cover the table with a pastel plaid or checkered tablecloth, or use an old quilt. Set a big stoneware crock of fresh flowers in the center. If the group is large, place the flatware in a basket where people can help themselves to the utensils.

Large pitchers of juice, platters of hickory-smoked bacon, cinnamon-and-oatmeal pancakes and maple syrup contribute to the homey feeling and provide the energy needed to get through this busy day.

Take time to relax and visit with your guests. You may be too caught up in the whirl of events to spend much time with them later in the day. Be sure to give equal time to every guest, as well as lots of hugs and kisses. Now's the time to load up the camera and take rolls of sentimental snapshots. Make plenty of copies to send to your guests after the wedding.

Bride's Brunch

Pity the poor bride with butterflies in her stomach. And what of her beleaguered mother? Chances are, neither one of them is much in the mood to eat ... but the wedding won't take place until late afternoon or evening. Make things easy on both of them by bringing in brunch for the whole family and the bride's attendants as well.

Set up an indoor picnic at the bride's home. Use a paper tablecloth, paper plates, napkins, and plastic utensils. Serve the fixings for cold sandwiches — meats, cheeses, breads, spreads — with a hot casserole and some raw vegetables and dip.

When the picnic's over, gather the dirty dishes, utensils and tablecloth and bundle them into a plastic garbage bag. Bid the bride adieu until you see her coming down the aisle.

If holding the brunch at the bride's home is inconvenient, invite the group to your home. At the party's conclusion, send the bride and her attendants to church in a rented limousine. It's a gesture she'll remember for years to come.

Slippin' and Slidin' Party _____

Few things are more delightful ice-skating across a frozen pond on a clear, 20-degree night, or swooshing down a snowy hill with a toboggan load of friends when the constellations are displayed across the darkened sky. If you live in a northern climate and you're having a winter wedding, why not organize an evening of outdoor winter activities? It's inexpensive, people of all ages can participate, and it will provide novel entertainment for wedding weekend guests who live south of the Mason-Dixon line.

Include an informal party note with your wedding invitation, or enclose an invitation you make yourself. Two pieces of construction paper cut in the shape of mittens and tied together with yarn will help you tell your guests everything they'll need to know.

Remind guests to bring warm clothes — long underwear, woolly socks, mittens, hats, and sweaters. (For fun, you may want to provide each guest with a scarf to wrap up in — in the bridal colors, of course!) They'll also need to bring their skates (if they have them), sleds, and toboggans.

Begin with an informal repast in your family room. Decorate the room with snowflakes cut from white or silver paper. Suspend them from the ceiling with transparent fishing line. Build a crackling fire in the fireplace or wood stove. Feed it pine cones dipped in waxes that give off different colors as they burn.

Place a bright red cloth on the buffet table. Place a large tureen in the middle of the table. Arrange soup spoons in a ray pattern around the tureen. Add baskets of crisp, crunchy crackers wrapped in checkered tea towels.

Fortify your guests with a dinner consisting of a hearty beef stew with corn meal muffins, or a hot, spicy chili.

After dinner, head for a nearby park that has a rink for skating and a hill for sledding. The frosty air will soon put a rosy glow on everyone's face.

Return home for some warming cups of hot chocolate topped with marshmallows or cinnamon-flavored whipped cream. Pop some popcorn in the fireplace, and chat about the wedding as the flames die down to embers.

Saturday Softball Tournament

Whip up some team spirit as you introduce his relatives to yours at a wedding weekend softball tournament between your two "teams."

Have T-shirts made for each team. Use white shirts for the bride's, colored shirts (perhaps the color of the attendants' clothes) for the groom's. Have the names of the bride and groom and the wedding date printed on the front.

Decorate the baseball diamond backstop with balloons and streamers and signs that say "Bill and Myra's Wedding Softball Tournament." Buy a set of inexpensive rubber bases from a sporting goods store. Paint the names of the bride and groom on each base. You may want to provide cheerleaders' pom-poms (in the bridal colors, of course!) for family members who are too young to play ball or simply don't want to jog around the bases.

Set out ice-filled coolers of beer and soft drinks so players and spectators can refresh themselves easily.

Start the game around 10:00 a.m. when everyone has lots of energy. When the game is over, have lunch at a nearby picnic area.

Weekend Kite-Flying Contest

Sometimes the simplest activities are the most fun. Organize a cross-generation kite-flying contest for some good, wholesome entertainment.

Take the gang to a local hill where the winds are good and the power lines are few. Write the names of the bride and groom on streamers and tie them to the kite tails. Award prizes for the kite that stays aloft longest and soars highest. Have a consolation prize ready for the one that gets away.

Then hike to a picnic area and have an old-fashioned wiener roast. When the coals are just right, roast some marshmallows. Make S'mores by sandwiching the toasted marshmallows between pieces of chocolate and graham crackers.

Wedding Wind-Down Party

If your out-of-town guests are staying at a hotel with pool facilities or if you happen to have a pool in your own backyard, wind down slowly with a pool party.

This type of party not only gives out-of-towners something to do, but it is a great way to get the clan together after the wedding. The warm water is sure to relax aching muscles. Kids who've been wearing their "dress-up" clothes all day long will appreciate the release.

Have some snacks and soft drinks on hand, and let the conversation drift along quietly after the kids have gone to bed.

Patriot Party

If your family is of a patriotic nature, and your daughter's wedding is in the summer, why not entertain everyone in a red-white-and-blue manner?

Begin with an impromptu children's parade the morning after the wedding. Grandparents can help the kids decorate their tricycles, bicycles, and wagons with red, white, and blue bunting and streamers. If you've given their mothers advance warning, the children can dress in Halloween costumes they've brought from home. Or let them raid the trunks in the attic for some dress-up fun.

After the kids have paraded around the block a few times, call the entire family group together for a flag-raising ceremony and photo session in the front yard.

Then retire to your bunting-draped backyard for a picnic. Place pots of red, white, and blue petunias along the fence. Play some John Philip Sousa marches on your cassette deck. Serve hot dogs, lemonade, and apple pie with homemade vanilla ice cream (have the kids take turns cranking the ice cream maker).

Day-After Picnic

You've just celebrated one of the biggest, most formal days of your life; your son or daughter has truly left the nest. Relax now with an informal picnic in a nearby park.

Choose a park that has playground equipment for little ones and a baseball diamond for older athletes.

If you're feeling tired, have the picnic catered. But it's much more fun if guests bring their favorite potluck dishes. It's also a great way to try out new recipes! Use paper plates and napkins and plastic eating utensils to make serving easy and keep cleanup simple.

This is an opportunity for the bride and groom to recount the excitement of their wedding. It also gives friends and family a chance to take last-minute photos, reflect on the events of the past few days, and send the pair off on their honeymoon. And you can sit back and catch up with the rest of the family!

Wedding Weekend Sightseeing Tour

Folks who are new in town are sure to appreciate this thoughtful gesture. Pack all your out-of-town guests into a van or tour bus and show them your area's points of interest.

Do the driving yourself, or arrange an excursion with a professional tour guide. In many cities, you can take tours with a set itinerary (such as a Grayline tour), or you can take a tour custom-tailored to the interests of your group. Some offer box lunches; others schedule a lunch stop along the way. Or, you may want to bring a deli lunch for your bunch.

Contact your state tourism department or your local convention and visitors bureau for information about tour operators in your area.

Sunday Send-Off

Send the bride and groom off on their honeymoon in style.

Begin with a champagne brunch in your backyard. Cover the picnic table with a white lace cloth, and put out your crystal serving dishes. Place a large basket filled with snapdragons, daisies, roses, or other flowers from your garden in the center of the table.

Serve a cracked wheat salad nestled in endive leaves. Follow up with sliced Virginia ham, baby vegetables, biscuits and honey, and elegant fruit tarts. Coffee and champagne complete the meal.

Decorate the yard with travel posters. If you can find them, use ones that depict the honeymoon destination.

Tie helium-filled balloons to the fence, to the trees, even to the backs of chairs. Release them as the couple departs. For extra fun, attach postcards (buy them already stamped from the post office) to the strings with your return address on the front and the names of the bride and groom and their wedding date on the back. Instruct finders to return the card to you, stating where the balloon came down and the date.

Don't forget to decorate the getaway car. Use more balloons, streamers, and tin cans. To protect the paint job on the groom's car, refrain from writing your message on the car with shaving cream. Instead, use computer-generated signs (available at many party supply stores) to tell the world that Tom and Lucy are "Just Married."

For a really special send-off, arrange to have the couple take off in a hot-air balloon. Have well-wishers follow the decorated car out to the field where the balloon will be launched, horns blaring all the way.

Allow plenty of time for last-minute hugs and kisses. Record the good-byes with your camera or VCR for a first-anniversary viewing.

12. Post-Wedding Parties

*T*he celebration doesn't have to end with the reception. It can continue through the night or in smaller parties during the weeks following the wedding.

Chivaree! ―――――――――――

The word *chivaree* comes from the French, *charivari*. The American Heritage Dictionary defines *chivaree* as a "noisy mock serenade to newlyweds." The word dates back even further to the Greek word *karebaria*, "heavy head."

Chivarees were once an all-night affair designed to prevent a widower who had married a much younger woman, or a widow who had remarried too hastily from consummating their union. In modern America, the chivaree has been reduced to a few cars following the bridal couple's getaway car, horns blaring and lights flashing. Why not revive the chivaree?

Go to a party supply store and gather up as many noisemakers, horns, and whistles as you can find. Dig up some old pots and pans and some wooden spoons to beat them with. Round up the couple's friends and relatives and conspire to have them meet at the hotel where the couple is staying.

If you have time, compose a little song or ditty especially for the occasion and teach it to the gang. If you're not blessed with musical talents, find a book of old, sentimental songs at your local library and copy the words out on a song sheet for your "choir." Include old chestnuts such as "Let Me Call You Sweetheart," "Down by the Old Mill Stream," and "By the Light of the Silvery Moon."

When everyone's huddled outside the couple's door or window, cut loose with a chorus or two — the more off-key, the better. Shake the rattles, blow the whistles, beat on the pots and pans. Although you may not keep the couple from the eventual consummation of their union, you will give them a night they'll remember every anniversary for years to come.

Remember, it's all in good fun. If the hotel manager asks your group to leave, do so politely.

After-the-Wedding Hometown Introduction _____

Logistics come into play when the bride hails from one city or state and the groom from another. Guests may not be able to make a long drive. For one reason or another, relatives may not be able to arrange a lengthy stay. For that reason, one couple found a dual celebration in order.

Invitations to the wedding with a church-parlor reception following the ceremony were issued to all guests. Accompanying the official invitation was an engraved invitation to a second reception held in the groom's hometown the day after the wedding. Guests were asked to return their R.S.V.P.s for either reception or both.

Both receptions were held at noon. Each had a different menu. The church reception had no alcohol, of course. Servings of wine and beer were offered freely at the second reception, which was held at a fine hotel. The groom's family hosted the second reception.

The wedding processional was re-enacted for the benefit of those who could not attend the ceremony. An announcer introduced the wedding party and the families of the bride and groom. A videotape of the wedding ceremony was played for the guests. Then, as a follow-up, a dance with a live band followed the dinner.

Although arranging dual celebrations such as these requires extra effort, time, and expense on your part, it signifies to your guests that their presence at your wedding is important to you. Guests who live far from the site of the wedding will appreciate your thoughtfulness and will make every effort to attend this second celebration.

Tip: If you are paying for the reception, make sure you make all the arrangements yourself to get complete satisfaction. To avoid confusion, make sure the hotel, country club, or restaurant discusses arrangements with only *one*, you or someone you designate as your spokesperson.

Post-Wedding Talent Show

Put your special talents to use when you entertain your out-of-town guests. If you've been taking tap or ballet lessons since childhood, treat your guests to a small-stage production of "I'm a Yankee Doodle Dandy." If you and your new husband are musicians, play a mini-concert of duets suited to your particular musical instruments. If you're actors, act out a scene from "Romeo and Juliet" or "Cyrano de Bergerac."

One bride, who was an accomplished puppeteer, presented a skit using puppets to represent the bride and groom. She used a regular puppet stage; you could easily construct one from a large cardboard box. Helium balloons were used as decorations. Although the skit was performed at her wedding reception, ice cream cones were served to the audience instead of wedding cake.

The puppets enacted the bride and groom's first meeting, and depicted several funny events leading up to their wedding. Guests appreciated the show, because it gave them insight into the couple's relationship and how it grew.

To make such an event even more fun for your guests, invite them to join you onstage for more play-acting, singing, and general horseplay.

Where to hold such a theatrical production? How about the park in the center of town? Use the bandstand as your stage, and decorate it with streamers and helium balloons. Spread blankets on the ground in front of the stage for your guests. Be sure to bring in folding lawn chairs for guests who may have a hard time lowering themselves to or raising themselves up from the ground.

Add to the theatrical atmosphere by offering popcorn, peanuts and soft drinks. Or serve a catered picnic lunch.

Long after the wedding is over, your guests will remember how you gave of yourself by providing some home-style entertainment for them.

Gift-Opening Party

Everyone loves getting presents. And it's almost as much fun to watch others open *their* gifts, too. To let everyone in on the fun, do what this couple did.

Invite your grandparents, aunts, and uncles to your new home to a gift-opening party. Give your relatives a tour of your home, then serve a light lunch. Give them a chance to "ooh" and "aah" over your gifts after eating.

Gift-opening parties can be held in your home, at the home of the bride's parents, or at the home of a member of the groom's family. If yours was a small wedding, and you have guests staying at a nearby bed and breakfast inn, arrange a gift-opening party at the inn. Have all the party guests assemble in the inn's dining room for a Continental breakfast, then open your packages. Be sure to have someone record the gifts and names of the givers so you can promptly send your thank-you notes.

The beauty of a gift-opening party is that it can be held at any time — immediately after the wedding, the following day, after the honeymoon — whenever it's convenient for you. Be sure to include important people such as grandparents, close friends, and certainly the members of your wedding party.

Presents in the Park

One couple chose a novel approach to the post-wedding gift opening by holding their party in a local park. It gave them a chance to spend more time with their families, and extended their celebration beyond the ceremony and reception.

Gifts that were brought to the home or wedding ceremony were loaded into a van. The day after the ceremony, the couple invited their friends and relatives to a picnic area which had been reserved for the group. A tent was set up so everyone could find the party location easily. A chauffeur was on call to shuttle guests to a dry place in case of rain. The gifts were brought by van to the park.

Young children, who weren't overly interested in the gifts, played on the playground equipment. Teenagers played volley-ball.

Their elders, who were tired from the wedding festivities, relaxed and watched the couple open the gifts. (Some napped.) Relatives pitched in to make this quiet celebration special. The aunts prepared salads while the uncles donned chef's aprons and cooked hamburgers and bratwurst over the grill.

A lazy afternoon in the park was a perfect way to wind down while spending time together as a family.

View-the-Gifts Wedding Brunch

For security reasons, many couples no longer open their gifts at the wedding reception. Guests never get a chance to see what's inside all the beautifully wrapped packages. Besides, the thoughtful couple gives their attention to their wedding guests, not to the presents.

Invite your guests to attend a post-wedding brunch at your home or at the home of your parents, and put the gifts on display.

Choose one area of the home in which to spread out the gifts. Make sure the cards are with the gifts so everyone can see that Aunt Betty gave you the crocheted tablecloth. If you receive duplicate gifts, display only one to spare your guests any embarrassment. It is not in good taste to display gifts of cash or checks. Simply place the cards on the table where people can read them if they so choose.

Serve a Continental breakfast of fresh juice, rolls, and coffee, or offer your guests a feast of quiche, croissants, and fresh fruit. Strawberries and champagne may also be served, if you are so inclined.

Guests will enjoy the opportunity to see your china pattern, the table linens and cooking utensils. They'll relish the chance to chat and reminisce about the wedding gifts they received years ago. Most of all, they'll appreciate being included in this post-wedding get-together.

Old-Fashioned Croquet Tournament

Wind down from the wedding and while away a summer's afternoon in an activity that will involve the very young and the very old — a croquet tournament.

Croquet is a game that can be played in a refined manner, or it can be fiercely competitive. It's a game that Grandpa can teach the grandchildren. Even teenagers will lose some of their customary boredom in the rivalry to be the first to reach the stake.

Set up the game on a large, level playing field. Line the course with lawn chairs for spectators. Split the group into teams, or play as individuals. Select one person to act as referee.

Fill helium balloons and use them to decorate the sidelines. Or hang paper honeycomb wedding bells in the trees. Tie narrow white velvet ribbons to the wickets and to the stakes at the ends of the field. Stencil the mallets with the names of the wedding couple, and tie a ribbon to each handle.

For refreshments, serve ice-cold lemonade and sugar cookies.

As the afternoon goes on, don't be surprised if the opposing teams become quite vigorous in defense of their territories and request a grudge match. Let the games begin!

European Morning-After Breakfast

If you've danced the night away at your son or daughter's wedding, you probably won't feel much like preparing breakfast the next morning. But you must look after your house guests.

Do as many Europeans do: Serve a breakfast buffet. Set out a variety of cereals and offer guests their choice of toppings such as brown sugar, canned sliced peaches, toasted coconut, sliced bananas, berries, dried fruits, granola, chocolate chips, canned mandarin oranges — even uncooked oatmeal! Have toast, jams, and jellies available, and serve plenty of orange juice and hot coffee.

If your guests like to eat hearty, follow the lead of the European hotels that cater to Americans and put out plates of cold salami, cheese, and bread.

Allowing your guests to serve themselves provides for their needs, while it relieves you of some of the burden of being a good hostess. It also reduces the uncomfortable feeling many guests have when their host or hostess waits on them hand and foot.

"Grazing" Party

First there was the rehearsal dinner. Then, the dinner at the wedding reception. After a day or two of formal dinners, visitors will appreciate the casual, come-as-you-are atmosphere of a Grazing Party.

For a gala but casual atmosphere, set up a buffet table with brightly-colored paper plates and napkins with coordinating plastic knives, spoons, and forks. If you have the energy, festoon the room with matching streamers, and toss confetti on the paper tablecloth.

Set out trays of assorted cheeses and crackers, crudités and dips, and a crockpot or two filled with chili or a favorite casserole. Pile a fruit bowl high with oranges, apples, and bananas. Pop some popcorn and scatter bowls of potato chips, pretzels, and peanuts around the room. Have plenty of coffee and soft drinks on hand, and let guests graze to their hearts' content.

The paperware will keep cleanup simple. When guests have snacked away the day, toss the dirty plates into a garbage bag. Remove the serving dishes from the buffet table, then roll the tablecloth into a ball and stuff it into the garbage, too. *Voila!* Instant cleanup!

Meet-the-Relatives Picnic _____

Inevitably, there is someone who can't make it to your wedding because of travel, illness, or previous plans. But that doesn't mean they can't share in your joy. A few weeks after the wedding, invite those relatives who sent their regrets to a picnic *in your new backyard.*

Have plenty of food and drink available for this informal gathering, but do most of the food preparation before your guests arrive. For example, partially bake a lasagna that you can pull out of the freezer and defrost in the microwave. Later, while it's baking, you'll be able to spend more time getting to know Uncle George and Aunt Sally.

A three-bean salad tastes better if it marinates overnight. Brownies freeze well. Green salads can be tossed ahead of time — and dressed at the last minute. The deli section of your supermarket may have garlic bread already buttered and seasoned and ready to pop into the oven or microwave. And, of course, gelatin must be made ahead of time.

To save time washing dishes, place food in storage containers that can also be used as serving dishes. For storing food in the refrigerator, shallow containers are better than deep containers; they permit the food to chill quickly, reducing the possibility of food poisoning. Paper plates and napkins and plastic utensils also cut down on the amount of time you spend washing dishes or loading the dishwasher.

Decorate ahead of time with a red-and-white tablecloth on the picnic table. Put flatware out in a wicker basket. You might like to use one that has separate compartments for knives, forks, and spoons and a pocket on the side for napkins. Use squeezable dispensers for condiments such as ketchup and mustard. For fun, tie red, white, and blue balloons in the trees.

With all these do-ahead ideas, you should be able to spend lots of time with your guests!

Newcomers' Progressive Dinner _____

There's nothing new about a progressive dinner — unless, of course, you're new in town. If you've just moved to your spouse's city, a progressive dinner provides a good opportunity to get to know your husband's friends and to visit their homes.

During a progressive dinner, couples "progress" from one course of the meal to another. Each family hosts a different course in their home. Beginning with the first course, guests work their way from house to house, to the last course —dessert and coffee. (A variation on this theme mixes up the courses so that dessert comes before the entree and soup is served last.)

The continuing change of scenery keeps the conversation going. Cooks get to try new recipes or show off a specialty. Because only one course is served at each household, there's no need for a massive cleanup effort at the end.

It's perfectly okay to use your casual dinnerware. An informal table setting with a nubby woven tablecloth or quilted place-mats are equally appropriate. Wooden napkin rings are just the right touch.

Don't be too stiff or formal. The idea is to have fun as you get to know one another.

If your group is spread out over a large metropolitan or suburban area, draw a map showing the location of each home on the dinner route, and use it as the cover illustration for your invitation. If the party will be hosted by the neighbors on your block, draw a series of rectangles next to a city street, and label the houses where the party will be held. Inside, include the purpose of the party — "Get to know your neighbors!" and the date. Then list the courses, locations, and the times each course will be served.

Be sure to allow plenty of time for visiting between each course since your friends will undoubtedly want to show off their homes. As the evening progresses, you'll be amazed at how your friendships progress, too!

Surprise-Announcement Party___

Perhaps it was a shipboard romance. Or a second marriage for both of you. Or maybe you just didn't want all the fuss and hassle of a big wedding. Even couples who have married quietly can bask in the good wishes of their friends and relatives.

Invite everyone to a party in your home. Then, when the group is all assembled, announce your marriage. Springing the good news on them gives you control of the situation and reinforces your decision to make a quiet beginning. It also eliminates the problem of asking guests not to bring gifts.

Cover your dining room table with a simple tablecloth. Set out your best china and silver and paper napkins printed with your name and the groom's. Serve wedding cake with champagne, punch, or coffee, or allow guests to help themselves.

You'll probably hear some good-natured scolding and exclamations such as "Why didn't you tell us?" Relax and accept everyone's good wishes.

13. Party Menus

*F*ollowing are suggested menus for selected wedding occasions mentioned in this book. They can be used as is, or as inspiration for your own party ideas.

――――――― ❧ ❧ ❧ ❧ ❧ ❧ ❧ ❧ ―――――――

An Intimate Affair

Spinach-and-Onion Salad
Crown Roast of Pork
New Potatoes in Butter and Chives
Orange-Glazed Carrots
Brandied Baked Apples

――――――― ❧ ❧ ❧ ❧ ❧ ❧ ❧ ❧ ―――――――

Patriot Party

Hot Dogs
Lemonade
Apple Pie with Homemade Vanilla Ice Cream

Summer Olympics Engagement Announcement Party

Grilled Hamburgers on Toasted Buns
Potato Salad
Corn on the Cob
Baked Beans
Watermelon

Look to the Future

Assorted Cheeses
Spicy Meatballs
Hungarian Goulash
Garlic Bread
Red Wine

Getting-to-Know-You Tea Service

Tea Sandwiches
Mints
Mixed Nuts
Coffee
Punch

Midwinter Beach Party

Barbecued Ribs
Hot Dogs
Potato Salad
Lemonade

Chocolataire

Hot Chocolate or Chocolate-flavored Coffee
Chocolate-covered Cherries
White and Dark Chocolate Truffles
Fudge
Chocolate Fondue
Fresh Pineapple, Strawberries and Marshmallows (for dipping)
Chocolate Cake, Chocolate Ice Cream, or Chocolate Mousse
Creme de Cacao

"Pink" Tea

Shrimp Salad
Watercress and Cream Cheese Sandwiches
Raspberry Sherbet or Frozen Strawberry Yogurt
Tea or Coffee

A Very Fitting Party

Fresh Asparagus Wrapped in Swiss Cheese, Ham and Pastry
Fresh Fruit.

Halloween Shower

Pumpkin Pie
Hot Apple Cider
Coffee

Western Shower

Chili
Baking Powder Biscuits

Mother-of-the-Bride Shower

Chicken Salad on Melon Wedges
Dinner Rolls
Lemon Mousse
Wine
Coffee

❧ ❧ ❧ ❧ ❧ ❧ ❧ ❧

Barbecue Shower

Barbecued Turkey Legs
Fruit Kebabs
Corn Grilled in the Husk

❧ ❧ ❧ ❧ ❧ ❧ ❧ ❧

Home Office Shower

Stuffed Mushrooms
Quiche
Muffins
Tossed Salad

❧ ❧ ❧ ❧ ❧ ❧ ❧ ❧

Groom's Bicycle Marathon

Fried Chicken
Cole Slaw
Biscuits

❧ ❧ ❧ ❧ ❧ ❧ ❧ ❧

Boys' Toys Shower

Assorted Cold Cuts and Cheeses
Salads
Dill Pickles
Breads and Spreads
Beer

Pirate's Beach Party

Shrimp Cocktail
Fresh Fish or Salmon Steaks
Rum Cake

❧ ❧ ❧ ❧ ❧ ❧ ❧ ❧

Heritage Rehearsal Dinner

(German)
Chicken Soup
Fried *Spätzle* Noodles
Roast Pork or Veal
Bread Pudding or Stewed Fruit Compote

(Irish)
Corned Beef with Cabbage
Turnips, Onions, Potatoes, Carrots and Parsnips
Irish Soda Bread
Jam Cake
Madigan's Velvet Trousers
Irish Coffee

(Scandinavian)
Baked Ham
Brown Beans
Assorted Cheeses
Rice Pudding
Pickled Herring
Sylta
Swedish Meatballs
Potatis korv
Krumkake
Coffee

Wedding Planning Party

Antipasto Salad
Spaghetti and Meatballs or Fettucini Alfredo
Garlic Bread
Chianti
Spumoni
Anise Cookies
Espresso

─────────── ❧❧❧❧❧❧❧❧ ───────────

Wild Game Rehearsal Dinner

Deer or Antelope Sausage
Assorted Cheeses
Smoked Pheasant
Wild Duck a l'Orange
Venison in Burgundy and Mushrooms
Wild Rice Pilaf
Green Beans Amandine

─────────── ❧❧❧❧❧❧❧❧ ───────────

Wedding Photo Party

Sparkling Water
Raw Vegetables
Sliced Apples
Crackers and Cheese

─────────── ❧❧❧❧❧❧❧❧ ───────────

Working Party

Sloppy Joes or Barbecued Ham on Buns
Corn Chips
Tossed Salad

Regional Buffet Bash

(Cajun)
Blackened Fish
Dirty Rice
Seafood Creole
Louisiana Bread Pudding

(New England)
Boston Baked Beans
Chicken Pie
Turkey with Oyster Stuffing
Cod Cakes
Indian Rye Bread
Colonial Wafers capped with Whipped Cream and Applesauce

(South)
Southern Fried Chicken
Corn Bread
Black-Eyed Peas
Biscuits and Red-Eye Gravy
Georgia Peach Pie

(Midwest)
Broiled Walleye
Wild Rice Pilaf
Blueberry Muffins

or

Prime Rib of Beef
Corn on the Cob

(Desert Southwest)
Pork Stew with Cornbread Stuffing
Baked Sea Bass with Cilantro Stuffing
Green Chili Stew with Lamb and Juniper Berries

Friday Night Fiesta

Nachos with Guacamole and Cheese
Margaritas
Tortillas
Enchiladas
Refried Beans
Sopaipillas and Ice Cream
Coffee with Brandy, Kahlua and Chocolate Syrup

Wedding-Morning Breakfast

Juice
Hickory-Smoked Bacon
Cinnamon-and-Oatmeal Pancakes
Maple Syrup

Slippin' and Slidin' Party

Hearty Beef Stew or Spicy Chili
Corn Meal Muffins
Crackers
Hot Chocolate with Marshmallows
or Cinnamon-Flavored Whipped Cream
Popcorn

Sunday Send-Off

Cracked Wheat Salad Nestled in Endive Leaves
Sliced Virginia Ham
Baby Vegetables
Biscuits and Honey
Fruit Tarts
Coffee
Champagne

View-the-Gifts Wedding Brunch

Fresh Juice, Rolls, and Coffee
or
Quiche
Croissants
Fresh Fruit
Strawberries and Champagne

❧ ❧ ❧ ❧ ❧ ❧ ❧ ❧

European Morning-After Breakfast

Choice of Cereals
(such as granola, muesli, corn flakes)
Choice of Toppings
(such as brown sugar, canned sliced peaches,
toasted coconut, sliced bananas, berries,
dried fruits, chocolate chips, granola,
canned mandarin oranges, and uncooked oatmeal)
Cold Salami, Cheese, and Bread
Toast, Jams and Jellies
Fruit Juice
Coffee

❧ ❧ ❧ ❧ ❧ ❧ ❧ ❧

Meet-the-Relatives Picnic

Lasagna
Three-Bean Salad
Brownies
Tossed Salad
Garlic Bread
Gelatin Salad

Alphabetical Listing of Party Themes

General Index

Cynthia Lueck Sowden is a native of Minneapolis, Minnesota. A graduate of the University of Minnesota School of Journalism, she worked for several years in public relations, where she planned press conferences and stockholders' meetings. A freelance writer and editor since 1984, she has produced several newsletters for the Minnesota chapters of Meeting Planners International and the Hotel Sales and Marketing Association. Her work with these two organizations has given her many contacts within the hospitality industry. She is a member of Women in Communications, Inc., and served as director of communications for the Twin Cities chapter in 1988. The hostess of many successful parties, she has included several of her own party themes in this book.

Available from Brighton Publications, Inc.

Games for Wedding Shower Fun by Sharon Dlugosch, Florence Nelson

Wedding Plans: 50 Unique Themes for the Wedding of Your Dreams by Sharon Dlugosch

Wedding Hints & Reminders by Sharon Dlugosch

Dream Weddings Do Come True: How to Plan a Stress-free Wedding by Cynthia Kreuger

Baby Shower Fun by Sharon Dlugosch

Games for Baby Shower Fun by Sharon Dlugosch

Kid-Tastic Birthday Parties: The Complete Party Planner for Today's Kids by Jane Chase

Romantic At-Home Dinners: Sneaky Strategies for Couples with Kids by Nan Booth/Gary Fischler

Games for Party Fun by Sharon Dlugosch

Reunions for Fun-Loving Families by Nancy Funke Bagley

An Anniversary to Remember: Years One to Seventy-Five by Cynthia Lueck Sowden

Folding Table Napkins: A New Look At a Traditional Craft by Sharon Dlugosch

Table Setting Guide by Sharon Dlugosch

Tabletop Vignettes by Sharon Dlugosch

Don't Slurp Your Soup: A Basic Guide to Business Etiquette by Betty Craig

Meeting Room Games: Getting Things Done in Committees by Nan Booth

Hit the Ground Running: Communicate Your Way to Business Success by Cynthia Kreuger

Installation Ceremonies for Every Group by Pat Hines

These books are available in selected stores and catalogs. If you're having trouble finding them in your area, send a self-addressed, stamped, business-size envelope and request ordering information from:

Brighton Publications, Inc.
P.O. Box 120706
St. Paul, MN 55112-0706

or call: 1-800-536-BOOK(2665)